AF480630

"Provides guidance on how to navigate your apprehensions during virtual team meetings, become more assertive, and communicate your ideas effectively."

— **Moshmi Sanagavarapu**
Group Director of Analytics, IPG Mediabrands

"Offers up Zen wizardry for your Zooms, ensuring bravos and encores on the virtual stage!"

— **Barbara Rubin**
Theater Director & Dialect Coach

"Whether you are new to online presentations or want to increase your 'virtual confidence,' this is the book to read."

— **Karen Abrams Gerber, EdD**
Founding Partner, Rally Point
for Collaborative Change, LLC

"Nancy Ancowitz's gentle yet powerful approach teaches you to transcend the limitations of screens and technology, creating intimate, meaningful relationships—even through a camera lens."

— **Adam Ma**
Product Development Executive

"Gives salient insight, specific, easily learned tools, as well as exciting new possibilities for the use of AI, that are sure to enhance all forms of online presentations."

— **Lisa Stathoplos**
Author of *Make Me* and
Chimera, A Shapeshifter's Journey

Praise for *Zoom to Success*

"Practical strategies to take control with confidence and have some fun along the way."

— **Kerry Hannon**
Bestselling Author of *In Control at 50+:
How to Succeed in the New World of Work*

"Like Waze for the chaotic world of virtual presentations."

— **Savio S. Chan**
Co-founder & CEO, American AI Leadership
Institute & Asian American Authors Book Club

"I highly recommend Nancy's book to ensure you are prepared, focused, and at ease for your next presentation!"

— **Paul Marrandino**
Head of Sourcing, Cloud Tech, Google

"Helps professionals find their voice and present with confidence, especially for those who don't see themselves as natural presenters."

— **Sarah Wheat**
Defense Industry

"Whether you're pitching ideas or leading teams, *Zoom to Success* helps you shine—and deliver with impact."

— **Michael Cole, PhD**
Principal Data Scientist at LexisNexis

"The definitive guide to feeling comfortable presenting—even when it is not comfortable at first."

— **Senia Maymin, PhD**
CEO Coach and Co-author of the
bestseller *Profit from the Positive*

"In Nancy's graduate business communication class at NYU, I learned how to turn nerves into confidence and communicate clearly in business settings. Now, in my career, I draw on those same lessons every time I present, lead a meeting, or interview online."

— **Tingting Zhou**
Compensation Expert

"Brings insight and humor to a staid yet important topic with practical tips to keep your audience engaged and allowing your expertise to shine through."

— **Nicole Woodard**
Executive Coach and Career Strategist

"Turns virtual dread into virtual edge."

— **Bryan Janeczko**
Health & Wellness
Entrepreneur and Innovator

"So needed in our expanding virtual world. Provides practical steps to guide introverts on the road to presentation success."

— **Jennifer B. Kahnweiler, PhD, CSP**
Author of *The Introverted Leader*

"As someone who leads teams and clients across virtual platforms, I find *Zoom to Success* an invaluable resource for building presence and confidence."

— Jiani Guo
VP of Revenue & Operations, SaaS Startup

"As one of Nancy's former grad students and now a quant researcher, I've carried her mantra, 'say more with less,' throughout my career. *Zoom to Success* channels that wisdom to the virtual stage—with clarity and sharp, practical tips."

— Tianci (Bill) Xu
Quantitative Researcher

"Brings Nancy's significant experience and expertise, deeply insightful and relatable wisdom, and actionable strategies to the challenging question of how we introverts can expand our capabilities beyond the bounds of our inherent tendencies to 'show up bigger' for any occasion."

— Dr. Gregory Lieberman
Cognitive neuroscientist
and "Future of Work" strategist

"Nancy enabled me to embrace the idea that focusing on small, simple, and sustainable steps leads to profound change."

— David Conn
CEO & Investor

"Must-have video-call guidelines for newbies and great reminders for the seasoned professional looking to improve."

— Mika Liss
CEO of SMB software & services
companies & Strategic AI Advisor

"I have never met Nancy in person, only via Zoom. So, there is every possibility that she is actually a virtual AI—except she is exquisitely aware of the foibles and fears of humans...so she must be one herself!"

— **Dewey Davis-Thompson**
Writer, Philanthropist and
the Original Internet Adept

"Relatable, well-conceived and researched guidance clad in an encouraging conversational style. Like a good, inspirational friend who once sat your seat only to rise gloriously from the detritus w shining insights."

— **C. M. Finley**

"Winning two major international fashion competitions wasn't just about the designs—it came down to how I presented my work to the judges...with Nancy's insightful guidance."

—**Marcia Patmos**
Founder & Creative Director, M.PATMOS

"Along with *Self-Promotion for Introverts*, *Zoom to Success* is the career strategy I have used to create my personal brand. I often turn Ancowitz's powerful and insightful lessons into actionable and executable bite-sized pieces."

—**Soo Lee-Finley**
Head of Model Risk Governance, Provident Bank

"My expertise is improvisation—Nancy seamlessly blends those skills into her advice."

— **Carl Kissin**
Master Improviser

"Offers actionable tactics to transform remote meetings and presentations from flat to fascinating, building on-screen confidence and competence."

— Julie Winkle Giulioni
Author of *Promotions Are SO Yesterday*

"Tackles serious business topics with ingenuity, wit, and humor, making this guide as engaging as it is useful."

— Nil Demircubuk, PhD
Author of *Down to Earth*

"Chock-full of helpful tips and powerful exercises developed through the author's experience and backed up with research."

— Michele Wucker
Author of *The Gray Rhino*

"As with Ancowitz's previous books, she offers a lot of practical, actionable advice, this time for nailing the virtual presentations that many professionals would rather avoid."

— Liz Colodny
Founder, Careersculpt.com

"The manual that should be included with every webcam."

— Ross Brand
Livestreaming Pioneer and Co-author
of *Video Podcasting Made Easy*

"Nancy Ancowitz is the real deal. She knows her stuff, knows how to coach with flair, and this book will help take your career to the next level!"

— Steve Orr
Author of *Podcasting for Small Business*

"Zoom to Success is next-level practical. Relatable and visceral to the core, it offers rare insights from someone who has "been there, done that" in a crowded, virtual world."

— **Mahesh Krishnamurti, CEO**
Thought Leadership Capital

"As someone who uses Zoom regularly for presentations, interviews, and online workshops and discussions and who has struggled with public speaking, how I wish I had this gem of a book years ago!"

— **Anne Newgarden**
Author of *Adventures of a Soul*

"Nancy Ancowitz's expert advice—covering everything from managing jitters to engaging distracted audiences—will help you show up with clarity, confidence, and authenticity in every online interaction."

— **Petter N. Kolm**
Professor, New York University

"Nancy is knowledgeable, passionate, and practical. Her guidance helps professionals find their voice and present with confidence, especially for those who don't see themselves as natural presenters."

— Chief of Talent Development and
Engagement, Defense and Government

ZOOM TO SUCCESS

PRESENT LIKE A PRO

ZOOM TO SUCCESS

PRESENT LIKE A PRO

by Nancy Ancowitz

University of
BRIDGEPORT PRESS
Bridgeport, Connecticut

Zoom to Success
by Nancy Ancowitz

Published by University of Bridgeport Press
126 Park Avenue, Bridgeport, CT 06604-7620

First Edition, December 2025

Design by Brian A. Dixon.

ISBN: 979-8-9935974-0-9

UNIVERSITY OF BRIDGEPORT PRESS
https://www.bridgeport.edu/

Contents

Foreword

by Mike Barlow

I read a lot of books about communication, leadership, and the art of getting your message across. Most of them overcomplicate things. They pile on frameworks, buzzwords, and endless lists of dos and don'ts—until the simple act of talking to another human becomes an obstacle course. This is not one of those books.

Nancy Ancowitz has written something refreshingly different. *Zoom to Success* is practical, human, and deeply encouraging. This book doesn't just tell you how to show up well in a virtual room—it shows you how to feel more like yourself when you do. And if there's one lesson we've all learned in recent years, it's that authenticity beats polish every time.

Nancy knows this terrain better than anyone. She's spent her career helping people—introverts, extroverts, and people of every stripe— find their voice and share it with the world. Her first book, *Self-Promotion for Introverts*, broke new ground by giving introverts a clear, confident path to career success. Now she's taking that same spirit and applying it to one of the most universal challenges of our time: how to present ourselves effectively online.

And let's be honest: virtual communication is not going away. Zoom, Teams, Meet, Webex—these aren't temporary stand-ins until the "real" world returns. They are the real world. They're the way we meet new colleagues, pitch ideas, land jobs, teach students, serve clients, and even connect with family. Being good at online presenting isn't an optional skill anymore. It's core to how we live and work.

I admire how Nancy demystifies that reality. She doesn't tell you to become someone you're not. She doesn't push TED-talk perfection or Instagram-ready backdrops. Instead, she offers clear, tested strategies that work in the messy, unpredictable flow of real life. Dogs bark. Wi-Fi hiccups. Slides freeze. Audiences drift. And yet, as Nancy reminds us, we still have the power to connect—if we prepare thoughtfully, stay grounded, and lean into our humanity.

Reading these pages, I kept underlining lines that felt instantly useful. Things like: *Your setup speaks volumes before you say a word.* Or: *Your jitters mean you care—channel that energy into delivery.* These aren't abstract slogans; they're field notes from someone who has been there, stumbled there, and ultimately thrived there. That's what makes this book credible: it's built on experience, not just theory.

Nancy's voice throughout is warm and encouraging, but also gently insistent. She wants you to succeed—and she won't let you off the hook with half-hearted effort. You'll find checklists, pro tips, cautionary tales, and yes, the occasional laugh-out-loud story about pink lemonade, sticky notes, and unmuted lunch orders. It's equal parts guide and companion, the kind of book you'll actually keep by your desk and use.

One of the most valuable aspects of *Zoom to Success* is its inclusivity. Nancy speaks directly to introverts, a group too often overlooked in the noisy world of professional communication. But she also broadens the frame, showing how extroverts, too, can benefit from structure, preparation, and mindful engagement. In doing so, she creates a toolkit for everyone—because everyone, regardless of personality type, feels a little vulnerable staring into that tiny camera lens.

I also appreciate Nancy's honesty about technology. She doesn't glorify it. She doesn't pretend every app is a silver bullet. She acknowledges that tools change, glitches happen, and the "perfect platform" is a myth. But she also points out that tech can be an ally if we use it wisely. From noise-reduction apps to AI rehearsal platforms, Nancy introduces tools in a way that feels empowering rather than overwhelming.

What really shines through, though, is her emphasis on connection. Over and over, Nancy reminds us that the goal of any presentation—virtual or otherwise—is to connect with people. To make them feel seen. To share something meaningful. To spark a conversation that matters. That's a radical message in a world where so much online interaction feels transactional.

Here's why that matters: Connection is the currency of our age. You can have brilliant slides, flawless lighting, and a voice that belongs on NPR—but if you don't connect, you've lost the room. Nancy teaches you how to win the room, not by dazzling it with tricks, but by grounding yourself in clarity, authenticity, and generosity.

That last word—generosity—is worth pausing on. At its heart, this book is about giving. Giving your audience your attention, your respect, your thoughtfulness, and yes, your best effort. Too many presenters think of virtual communication as a performance. Nancy reframes it as an act of service. And when you approach it that way, the pressure eases. You're no longer proving yourself; you're sharing yourself.

I'll go one step further: this book is more than a manual for presenting online. It's a quiet manifesto for better communication in every aspect of our lives. Imagine what our workplaces, classrooms, and even our families could be like if we all applied Nancy's advice—listening more closely, speaking more clearly, and showing up more authentically. That's not just presentation advice. That's life advice.

If you're reading this book right now, I want to encourage you to dive in with curiosity. Don't skim it like a manual you'll never open again. Read it the way you'd listen to a trusted friend who's figured out a tricky skill and is now walking you through it, step by step. Try the checklists. Experiment with the techniques. Reflect on the insights. And most of all, let yourself relax into the idea that you *can* do this.

Nancy's greatest gift as a teacher is not just her technical expertise—it's her belief in people. She sees potential where others see anxiety. She sees clarity where others see chaos. And she sees possibilities where others see only obstacles. That spirit animates every page of this book.

Nancy's book will be assigned reading in most of the courses I teach at the University of Bridgeport, and I'm looking forward to using it in the classroom!

So, here's my invitation: Read this book. Use it. Share it. Let it nudge you out of procrastination and into action. And the next time you're staring at your own face on Zoom, mic checked and ring light ready, you'll remember Nancy's words: You don't need to be perfect. You just need to be present.

That's a message worth carrying—not just into your next meeting, but into your life.

About Mike Barlow

Mike Barlow is the author of *Learning to Love Data Science* (O'Reilly), and coauthor of *Smart Cities, Smart Future* (Wiley), *The Executive's Guide to Enterprise Social Media Strategy* (Wiley) and *Partnering with the CIO* (Wiley). He is the author of more than a dozen O'Reilly Reports, including the prophetic *Practical AI in the Cloud* and *The Culture of Big Data*. He teaches popular classes in public communications and professional writing at the University of Bridgeport in Bridgeport, Connecticut. Mike is an engaging and energetic teacher and speaker.

Note on Use of Generative AI

I drew on my deep professional experience in online presenting to write this book. Along the way, I used generative AI tools (including ChatGPT, Perplexity, and related models) as creative partners: to spark brainstorming, suggest different ways to frame key topics, and assist with verifying factual accuracy. Every judgment call, personal reflection, and practical recommendation in these pages is my own.

Introduction

Your online presentation starts in 15 minutes. You're facing your own anxious reflection on Zoom, making "eye contact" with your laptop's camera, fixing your posture—and, of course, practicing that winning genuine smile. You're sure your content is crap, and you are not at all happy with your slides.

Meanwhile, the always-ready overachievers beam in with perfect angles, artful lighting, and backgrounds so pristine you feel as if you're dialing in from a broom closet while they're broadcast-ready for TED.

If you've ever felt like that—welcome.

Let's face it: Presenting online can feel like launching your best ideas into the cyber-void—blank stares, silence, boredom, and an audience who seems elsewhere. I know, because I've been guilty myself of checking email, skimming headlines, and finally booking that overdue haircut mid-webinar.

Not proud. But your audience? They're often right there with me—or worse. (Cue the guy yelling his lunch order, unmuted. Extra pickles.) But the good news? Even a distracted crowd can be captivated. You can break through, spark attention, and actually connect—if you know how.

I didn't start out cool on camera. Early on, I was all nerves and second-guessing, convinced everyone was born for this but me. Improvisation classes gave me the guts and skills to think on my feet and speak up—

even when my inner introvert just wanted to stay quiet. I made every mistake there is. But flop after flop, I figured out what lands.

The more I remembered what I actually brought to my online presentations—my distinct point of view, real experience, a desire to help others—the more I could focus on what mattered, reaching my audience.

I know firsthand that what sets you apart isn't perfection—it's showing up as yourself: real, present, ready. Whether you're pro-level or it's your first day, this book is your fast-track to virtual confidence, natural connection, and reliably making things work—Zoom, Teams, Meet, Webex, and all. Even when your audience drifts or isn't fully present, you can keep them engaged and invested.

I had to learn the hard way how to stop sweating and start connecting, but you don't have to. This book will spare you hours of trial and error and arm you with strategies for dealing with Murphy's Law, meaning, if anything can go wrong, it will—usually mid-presentation.

What you'll learn

Virtual presentations come with special challenges: talking into a camera, troubleshooting tech meltdowns mid-sentence, and engaging an audience you can't always see. Add in the demands of virtual meetings and job interviews, and the pressure only increases. This book cuts through the noise with practical strategies, clear examples, and quick wins for preparation, set-up, and your online presence.

Zoom to Success will help you:

- Navigate presentation jitters with confidence.

- Set up a distraction-free virtual stage.

- Engage your audience with clarity, energy, and authenticity.

- Prevent and handle tech mishaps like a pro.

- Lead and participate effectively in virtual meetings—including tips for acing virtual job interviews.

- Use AI tools for everything from preparing your content to helping you rehearse.

- Succeed as an introvert, by preparing strategically and learning a few improvisation hacks.

This book will help you connect with your audience, keep tech gremlins in check, and shine in meetings and interviews. The result? Presentations that are meaningful, memorable, and worth everyone's time. You'll also find actionable tips throughout the book for creating visually engaging materials, so your slides support your message and keep your audience focused.

Pro tip

Nothing replaces actually giving online presentations—doing, rather than just reading about doing. But if you're going to procrastinate, reading this book could nudge you in the right direction!

What your audience wants

Research suggests that online, what matters most isn't slick production values but how clearly and authentically you connect. Bailenson (2021) adds that much of video-call fatigue comes from nonverbal overload—constant eye contact, self-view, and restricted movement—rather than surface-level tech issues. Your audience values clarity, relevance, and authenticity over fireworks. Virtual success comes from commanding attention, earning trust, and addressing distractions head-on. Throughout this book, you'll find tailored strategies for introverts and those who work with them, AI tools to enhance preparation and delivery, and techniques that help you transfer virtual skills to in-person presentations.

How to use this guide

Here's how to get the most out of what's ahead: Each chapter focuses on one essential skill or topic, with straightforward tips and tools designed to save you time. Each one stands alone so you can dive straight into the sections that matter most to you. Start at the beginning if you're looking to create a professional virtual setup—or skip ahead to polish specific skills like audience engagement, vocal delivery, troubleshooting, or leading effective meetings.

Tech tool disclaimer

Tech evolves quickly. The tools in this book reflect what worked well at the time of writing. I haven't personally road-tested every tool I mention; they come from a wide range of sources including colleagues, clients, peers, faculty ed-tech sessions, trusted articles, and even AI-driven searches. Some are free and some have paid plans, so choose what fits your style and budget. Since features shift and trends change, I encourage you to check the latest reviews before diving in.

And remember: the "best" tech is the one that helps you feel prepared and present, not necessarily the newest or flashiest thing.

How this book dovetails with my others

Zoom to Success complements my recent guide, *Business Writing: Say More with Less* (2024)—a book packed with actionable insights—and

Introduction

my earlier work, *Self-Promotion for Introverts*® (2009), among the first books to bring introvert-friendly career strategies into the mainstream conversation.

While *Business Writing* focuses on clear communication in writing and *Self-Promotion for Introverts*® addresses career promotion from an introvert's perspective, this guide translates those principles into the realm of virtual presentations, meetings, and interviews. Whether you're presenting online or in person, you'll find strategies to connect, captivate, and communicate effectively—with special attention to helping introverts thrive and to supporting those who want to better understand them.

While my journey is through the lens of a highly sensitive introvert, the strategies here support all presenters—no matter your personality. I offer a variety of tools and approaches you can mix and match to build your own personal presentation toolkit—so you can find what works best for you.

Ready to command the virtual stage, ace your next meeting, and shine in virtual interviews? Let's dive in! So, the next time you're staring down your own reflection—mic checked, ring light ready— you'll know exactly how to turn that countdown into your launch moment. (And just imagine: One day, those squares on your screen will become full-blown 3D holograms, where eye contact means sharing space with lifelike digital colleagues. But that's a story for another time—or maybe another dimension altogether.)

Next up—Chapter 1: Set the Virtual Stage

Your virtual environment sets the tone for your entire presentation. A cluttered background, poor lighting, or tinny audio can sink your message before you say a word. In Chapter 1, we'll cover how to create a polished virtual stage that helps your message land and boosts your credibility from the moment you go live. You'll learn how to look, sound, and feel prepared—without needing a studio budget.

Reference

Bailenson, J. N. (2021). Nonverbal overload: A theoretical argument for the causes of Zoom fatigue. *Technology, Mind, and Behavior*, 2(1).

Chapter 1

Set the Virtual Stage

We've all been there. You're delivering an online presentation and everything's smooth sailing—until your audio cuts out, your video freezes, or a jackhammer crew creates a street symphony outside your window. These snags are inevitable, but a little savvy prep goes a long way toward sidestepping most of them.

I've come to expect some version of Murphy's Law whenever I present online. Just yesterday, everything worked perfectly during the tech check for a workshop. I met 30 minutes before showtime with the client's point person, and we tested everything twice over. But when we went live? My screen share crashed—yikes, gulp—but thankfully, the client had backup slides. So, even with careful prep, tech gremlins invariably find a way to sneak in.

Setting up for an online presentation can make me a bit of a jumping bean—nerves and the pressure to nail every detail sometimes collide and threaten to knock me off my stride. What grounds me is carving out an hour for focused prep: a deep breath, a methodical checklist. That hour transforms chaos into calm; I'm ready to turn frenzy into connection.

I remind myself to slow down and breathe deeply, which sharpens my focus and clears my head when things get bumpy. Beats panicking and sinking into technical-glitch quicksand. When the jitters hit anyway? That's what Chapter 2 is for.

Online presentations have become a staple of the business world, and they come with their own set of curveballs, from gear on the fritz to distracted audiences (Bailenson, 2021). But they offer an invaluable chance to show up authentically and connect across any distance. You can instantly reach people in all corners of the globe, something impossible in person. This chapter will help you set the stage for an online presentation space that supports your message and draws your audience in.

A tale of two presenters

🚫 Presenter A: The tech trainwreck

Your face is tucked in shadow like a Hitchcock villain, your background cluttered with last week's laundry, and your audio sounds like you're speaking from the bottom of a well. Instead of delivering your big moment, you're trapped in your own low-budget thriller—every off-kilter camera angle, echo, and awkward pause building toward a foregone conclusion. Still, you have your script and stay on it because you know what you want to say. Like a cornered villain who knows the credits are about to roll, you grip your script and plow through, just wanting this thing to be over before the final fade-out.

✅ Presenter B: The virtual virtuoso

You appear on screen sharp and composed, framed by a tidy, neutral background. Your audio is crisp, clear, and inviting. Before launching in, you warmly greet the group, mentioning a recent team win or referencing a quick chat you had with a couple of participants. This timely, relevant connection draws listeners in and signals that you see and value them as people, not just faces in a grid. Your setup is your spotlight in the virtual world, grabbing attention and conveying credibility (Hall, Pennington & Wang, 2023). You start and end on time and use every minute in between to keep the group's attention where it belongs—on a conversation worth showing up for. That's how you hold the digital room from the first hello to the last goodbye (the ubiquitous Zoom wave included).

Your online setup checklist

Use this checklist to polish your virtual stage:

- **Location:** Find a spot that says "professional"—think home office or a quiet corner of your living room. Avoid high-traffic zones and put a sticky note on the door or shoot a heads-up text to others to minimize interruptions. If you share your space with kids or animals, put plans in place to minimize surprise appearances.

- **Background:** Choose a neutral, uncluttered physical backdrop or virtual background. If appropriate, use your organization's logo for a sleek touch. Organization logos add polish. A tropical backdrop only works if you're truly in Bali.

- **Lighting:** Use two light sources from the front or sides for balanced, flattering light. Face a window during the day; use a lamp for evenings or cloudy skies. Skip overhead or backlighting that creates unwanted shadows—unless you're angling for the part of Mysterious Alien #2.

- **Audio:** Test your microphone for clear sound— no static or echoes. Your audience should hear your insights, not your ambient sound. Most video platforms offer noise suppression or reduction settings—enable these to minimize passing ambulances, leaf blowers, and even A/C units. Noise-reduction apps like Krisp or built-in filters work wonders. For best results, use an external mic and mute anything that could be distracting.

- **Camera angle:** Center yourself in the frame with your shoulders visible, and a bit of space above your head. Position your webcam at eye level; stack books under your laptop if needed. Sitting too low or too high can distract your audience. If you're in a swivel chair, resist the urge to pivot—even small movements can pull attention away from your message. Also, clean your camera lens; make sure your internal computer lighting is up and not creating a dimly lit atmosphere.

- **Tech check:** Join about 15 minutes early to test audio, video, and screen share. I even log in up to an hour early, step away to center myself, and return focused. A final "Testing, testing...is this thing on?" ensures peace of mind.

- **Internet:** Aim for a strong, stable internet connection—wired is best. If using WiFi, sit close to your router and consider a WiFi extender.

- **Your look:** Choose clothing that contrasts with your background and avoid busy patterns or blinding colors. Most online presentations frame you from the chest up, so keep visible attire neat and professional. Quick mirror or camera check for flyaways or smudges builds confidence.

💻 Rookie mistakes—DON'T:

- Overload with online backgrounds; DO favor simple visuals with plenty of "white space."

- Neglect accessibility; DO use tools like Microsoft's Accessibility Checker to check contrast and font sizes, ensuring slides are readable for people with visual impairments.

- Ignore lighting; DO make sure your lighting looks professional so as not to alienate your audience.

- Skip tech checks; DO prepare your tech setup; it's as crucial as rehearsing your content.

- Wing your setup; DO revisit your environment daily since lighting, noise, and connectivity can change.

 In-person presentation strategies

Project your voice for the room, make deliberate eye contact with one person at a time (about three seconds each), and square your shoulders—imagine if you and your audience both put your arms in front, you'd form parallel tracks. When making eye contact, rotate your whole torso, not just your head, for confident connection. Always check both in-room and virtual tech ahead; small adjustments matter.

Facilitating online meetings

If you're leading a virtual meeting (versus a presentation), much of this chapter applies. Your audio/visual setup shapes how others perceive you. Set clear agendas, manage time and voices fairly, keep the tone welcoming. More in Chapter 10: Ace Virtual Meetings and Interviews.

Tech tools

Try these to elevate your game:

- **External microphone and webcam:** Use affordable external devices to consistently deliver crisp sound and sharp video

- **Lighting:** Budget-friendly LED ring lights or strategically placed desk lamps brighten your image and minimize shadows

- **AI presentation simulators:** Tools like VirtualSpeech let you rehearse in immersive settings, from boardrooms to conference stages, with built-in AI feedback on delivery (e.g., pacing) and content. They're not a replacement for rehearsing with humans, but they offer a low-stakes opportunity to practice and get objective feedback when no colleague is available.

Introvert insights

Sometimes I feel unmoored without my notes—even if I know my content cold. Sticky notes around my screen are my go-to: they highlight key points and reminders. Think of them as your private cue cards—subtle confidence boosters just out of frame.

I like to carve out an hour before presenting to get mentally grounded and ready. However, the tech check itself usually takes just 10–15 minutes, depending on factors like platform, complexity, and fussiness of the setup. Personal and tech prep each have their place and both feed into smart readiness.

By fine-tuning your virtual environment, you create a welcoming space that builds your confidence as a speaker and keeps people involved. This helps extroverts, too—while they may be comfortable speaking spontaneously, a polished setup gives them a stable foundation that supports focus and helps them stay on message. For everyone, trial and error is the best way to discover what smart prep means for you.

Picture this: Sticky notes, soft light, and pink lemonade

I reviewed my slides, sticky notes lined my screen, natural light on one side, soft lamp on the other. Laptop elevated, webcam eye level. Tech check with my host—no rushing. Five minutes to breathe, stretch, sip pink lemonade (to match my sticky notes!).

Participants join. I smile, focusing on the value I'll deliver, not their judgments. My nerves? I channel them into excitement for the challenge. People nod, stay off email, and stay with me. I haven't just set the stage; I've become it, and it's paying off.

You don't need a production crew—just some thoughtful choices: where you sit, lighting, sound, tech prep. Your setup isn't just a backdrop; it actively shapes how your audience receives your message.

Pro tips

- **Log in early:** Join about 15 minutes beforehand for tech check and buffer time for glitches.

- **Backup plans:** Keep everything charged and have backup devices and alternative internet at hand. Major events merit extra gear; regular meetings need only solid connections.

- **Wingperson:** Arrange for someone (in advance) to handle chat, polls, or step in for technical hiccups

💡 The big idea

Your setup speaks volumes before you say a word. A thoughtfully prepared virtual stage signals professionalism and shows respect for your audience. Recent studies confirm: effective setups lead to higher engagement, trust, and speaker credibility (Hall, Pennington, & Wang, 2023). Think of it as a bonus: a setup that works for your audience often works for your nerves, too.

Next up—Chapter 2: Manage Presentation Jitters

Even when I look calm on camera, nerves can mean a sleepless night or a few silly mistakes. Whether you're anxious or seeking sharper delivery, Chapter 2 will help you channel those butterflies and give your best, every time.

References

Bailenson, J. N. (2021). Nonverbal overload: A theoretical argument for the causes of Zoom fatigue. *Technology, Mind, and Behavior*, 2(1).

Hall, J. A., Pennington, N., & Wang, Y. (2023). Video conferencing communication: Effects on trust, engagement, and audience perception of speakers. *Journal of Virtual Communication*, 5(3), 120–138.

Note on spelling: In this book, I use extroversion for readability. In academic psychology and Myers-Briggs Type Indicator® literature, extraversion is the preferred spelling.

Chapter 2

Manage Presentation Jitters

What's your biggest fear about presenting online? For me, it's gnawing perfectionism—the compulsion to check my slides until my eyes glaze over like donuts and I end up just sitting and staring blankly at the screen. I've spent way too many hours obsessively proofreading. I've tweaked fonts, hunted phantom typos, and debated whether "optimize" or "maximize" was more on-brand. Sound familiar?

But here's what all that editing-induced eye strain taught me: Perfect slides won't save you. What truly matters is connection; showing up authentically, sharing insights that resonate, and telling stories that stick in minds like catchy lyrics you can't shake. Your jitters are simply your body gearing up to connect deeply—so notice them, then let your true self take the stage.

If you suffer from presentation jitters, you're far from alone—they are reported by up to one third of the population (Ebrahimi et al., 2019). From my perspective, online presentations can amplify nervous energy because those framed faces often feel closer on the screen than they do in person. What helps me is preparing thoroughly, centering myself, and then getting out of my own way. How? By remembering I'm here to serve my audience—rather than awaiting barbs from my scalding, self-appointed critics. Life. Argh.

Why jitters strike—and why they don't mean you're doing it wrong

Maybe you worry about boring your audience—a fear my clients mention more than others. They also worry about fumbling with tech or feeling like they're speaking into vast nothingness. Though your rational brain knows these fears won't destroy you, your primal brain is sure you're being hunted by lions.

Let's turn those glazed eyes into laser focus. Through coaching thousands of clients and grad students—and facing down my own stage fright—I've learned that managing jitters is less about pretending to be fearless and more about reframing your nervousness, prepping like a pro, and finding your own rhythm. After all, nervousness means you care. Let it sharpen your focus rather than derail it.

Mindset tricks—from research and recommendations

Science to the rescue: How you frame your nerves changes their impact. Instead of thinking, I'm so anxious, try telling yourself, I'm excited to share this. Studies show this mental pivot boosts performance by 22% (Brooks, 2014). It transforms nerves into energy that works for, not against, you.

Another powerful trick? Talk to yourself in the second or third person. Instead of "I'm excited to share this," try "You're excited to share this," or "Nancy is excited to share this." Research shows second- or third-person self-talk helps regulate emotions better under pressure (Kross et al., 2014).

The upshot? The next time your jitters creep in, say: "You're excited to give this presentation," or "Nancy is excited." Awkward at first? Stick with it—it works. I've also heard self-improvement gurus say to do affirmations while looking in the mirror. I can't do the mirror-affirmation thing with a straight face, so I'll say my piece, then make a ridiculous face at myself just to break the tension. Still, mirror affirmations might work for you.

You can also experiment with time-tested ways to tame your nerves and release tension. Some of my clients and grad students also like shaking out their hands really fast to release trapped energy. Some do neck rolls and full body stretches. Others seem to enjoy making horse lips and funny sounds. Discover what works for you.

Why virtual presenting can feel harder—and how to make it easier

Virtual presentations can crank stress up even more than in-person speaking. Recent research shows that social anxiety readily extends to videoconferencing situations, often heightened by features unique to online platforms, such as constantly seeing your own image and the reduced ability to read nonverbal cues. These factors can make nerves feel just as sharp—or sharper—online as they do on stage (Russell, Hale, Eible, & Fisak, 2024). The good news? It's in your power to channel that adrenaline into a dynamic presentation.

A tale of two presenters

🚫 Presenter A: The nervous novice

Your coffee mug trembles as you take a sip—bad idea. For many people, me included, caffeine and nerves don't mix. You glance at your audience, but those Zoom squares feel massive and judgmental. Your heart races. Your mind goes blank. Your panic spikes like a bad WiFi signal when you forget your key point.

 Presenter B: The confident communicator

Now imagine the opposite, starting strong. You've rehearsed, used proven breathing techniques, and reframed your anxiety as excitement. The tech is working. Your slides are ready. Your energy is focused. You zero in on delivering value to your audience. If you forget a key point, you realize you're human. You glance at your notes, work it in later, or follow up by email—and the audience still leaves feeling informed and involved.

The better you know what works for your body and mind, the more confidently you'll command your virtual stage.

Jitter busters: Quick-fix strategies that work

Start with a two-minute reset: inhale for four counts, hold for four, and exhale for eight. Your shoulders will thank you. Skip the caffeine if it spikes your anxiety—but if coffee helps you focus, go for it. The key: Know what works for your body, which takes trial and error. Either way, sip some water too—it keeps your voice clear and gives you a moment to pause.

Build your confidence by recording a short segment. Instead of nitpicking, focus on what you do well. Share the clip with a trusted friend for feedback. Finally, place three key points on a sticky note by your camera. Some of my clients like that—if only for the extra hit of security.

⌨ Rookie mistakes—DON'T:

- Memorize every word; DO focus on key points and smooth transitions instead.

- Skip practice; DO rehearse out loud.

- Hold your breath when nervous; DO take deep breaths to keep you grounded.

- Chase perfection over connection; DO focus on engaging your audience, which matters most.

🎬 In-person presentation strategies

Managing nerves in the room

Online, you can clutch a stress ball under your desk. In person? You are the stress ball. No mute button, no camera-off option, no pretending your WiFi cut out. But here's the secret: nerves aren't your enemies. They can fuel your energy, sharpen your focus, and make you more engaging—if you know how to manage them (Brooks, 2014).

You now have a stage or room to command. Visit it beforehand if possible. Stand where you'll speak, adjust your setup early, decide whether to move or anchor at the lectern. I usually prefer moving— unless a camera locks me in.

True voice projection comes from breath support, not volume. Place your hand on your stomach—if it moves with your breath, you're doing it right. If your throat tires quickly, you're forcing it. Instead, pick a spot at the back of the room and project your voice to it.

In person, it's easier to feel audience energy right away. Take a breath to steady yourself before starting. Make eye contact with friendly faces (or their foreheads if it's easier). Don't fear pauses; silence signals poise, not panic.

Channel nervous energy into movement—on screen and on stage

If your nerves show up physically, don't fight them—use them. Whether you're presenting online or in person, let your hands rest naturally or gesture with intention. Online, keep movements within the camera frame and avoid fidgeting. In person, plant your feet hip-width apart and move deliberately—step forward to emphasize a point; don't pace. Pacing diffuses your energy and can make you just look nervous. Your movement becomes presence when it's purposeful. Once you center yourself, it's easier to think clearly and speak with intention.

Tech tools

These tools boost prep, poise, and presence:

- **Virtual rehearsal platforms:** Tools like Virtual-Speech and Yoodli simulate real presenting conditions and give feedback on pacing and filler words. These platforms are well-reviewed, offer AI-powered analysis, and include features like roleplay scenarios and instant suggestions.

- **Recording apps:** Loom and Zoom let you record and self-coach presentations. Loom is user-friendly with some audio glitches noted, Zoom is reliable with strong video and audio quality and widely used.

- **Breathwork and meditation:** Calm, Headspace, and Insight Timer provide pre-presentation meditations and breathing exercises. Calm is praised for variety and sleep stories. Headspace is beginner-friendly but can feel repetitive. Insight Timer offers an extensive

free   meditation   library   with   community
features.

Introvert insights

Introverts often find strength in deep preparation—it grounds us and helps us face the spotlight with greater calm. But make no mistake: introversion doesn't automatically make you a better preparer; it just makes preparation more essential for us. Many introverts, myself included, tend toward perfectionism. Some extroverts struggle with it, too.

Research shows a strong link between perfectionism and social anxiety, including presentation anxiety. Perfectionists set very high standards for themselves and fear falling short, which can lead to paralysis rather than productive preparation. This combination often results in a double-edged sword: perfectionism keeps us striving to meet excellent standards but can also cause us to freeze or procrastinate when those standards feel unattainable or even cruel (National Library of Medicine, 2022).

For introverts, this dynamic might look like excessive rehearsing, over-editing slides, or obsessing over every slide detail—behaviors born of wanting to control the outcome in a situation that feels inherently uncertain. While thorough preparation is powerful, excessive perfectionism can drain energy, increase stress, and ultimately reduce presentation effectiveness. Embracing your introverted nature and managing perfectionism effectively lets your authentic voice come through, turning nervous energy into a poised, confident presentation style that resonates.

And if you're an extrovert? Your fuel is interaction. Use the chat, polls, or quick audience participation to keep that energy loop flowing—just be mindful not to exhaust your introvert listeners in the process. It's all a balancing act.

Picture this: Shake, sip, and shine

Ten minutes before showtime, my foot's tapping like it's auditioning for the Off-Broadway musical "Stomp." I take a sip of water, roll my shoulders, and glance at the sticky note beside my camera: "Serve, don't impress."

My tech is checked, and my slides are fine—but my real prep is mental. As the virtual room begins to fill, I reframe the jitters: they're just my brain handing me bonus energy. By the first minute, my hands have stopped fidgeting and started illustrating. My voice evens out. Someone smiles, then nods. Just like that, the jitters become momentum.

Pro tip

Nerves can actually boost your performance. Treat them like energy that you can redirect—not as signals that you're unprepared (Brooks, 2014). Embrace your own rituals if they help—whether that's taking a quick dance break, doodling a funny face, squeezing a stress ball, pacing in socks like a pre-game coach, or running through a silly tongue-twister to wake up your voice. (Wait, where exactly does Sally sell those seashells?!?)

♀ The big idea

Presentation jitters don't mean you're unprepared—they mean you care. Channel that energy into a delivery that feels alive. So, take a deep breath, step into your power, and let your authentic and centered self take the reins. Your audience is waiting—and more than likely, rooting for you!

Next up—Chapter 3: Create Compelling Content

In the next chapter, we'll tackle how to shape your message for clarity, engagement, and impact.

References

Brooks, A. W. (2014). Get excited: Reappraising pre-performance anxiety as excitement. *Journal of Experimental Psychology: General*, 143(3), 1144–1158.

Ebrahimi, O. V., Pallesen, S., & Kenter, R. M. F. (2019). Psychological interventions for the fear of public speaking: A meta-analysis. *Frontiers in Psychology*, 10, Article 488.

Kross, E., Bruehlman-Senecal, E., Park, J., Burson, A., Dougherty, A., Shablack, H., & Ayduk, Ö. (2014). Self-talk as a regulatory mechanism: How you do it matters. *Journal of Personality and Social Psychology*, 122(1), 61–82.

Russell, M., Hale, N., Eible, A., & Fisak, B. (2024). The measurement of videoconferencing anxiety and avoidance. *Technology, Mind, and Behavior*, 5(4).

National Library of Medicine. (2022). The relationship between perfectionism and social anxiety. National Center for Biotechnology Information.

Chapter 3

Create Compelling Content

For most online presentations, including meetings and interviews, a strong delivery rests on three legs, like a sturdy stool: content, voice, and body language. This chapter focuses on the first leg: crafting strong content and explaining why a solid foundation is essential. Clear, compelling content supports everything else by building trust, earning attention, and creating impact.

If you're anything like me, preparing for a virtual presentation can look more like toggling between slides and a dozen open tabs (wait—what's that outrageous new diet hack that promises I'll never die?!?). Sometimes my perfectionism dresses up as productivity—tweaking slides, Googling endlessly, chasing the illusion that one more edit will make everything just right.

But all that busywork can pull me away from what really matters: connecting with my audience and delivering real value. That's what this chapter is about.

Distractions always lurk in the background—ready to derail me at the slightest opening. I've been known to wander into the kitchen and end up forearm-deep in a bag of peanut butter pretzels, momentarily convinced they count as protein to justify the grab. Technically, they sort of do—but probably not enough to guarantee immortality.

Confession: When I'm preparing for a virtual presentation, my perfectionism often masks my deeper doubts. I often struggle with what content to include. It quickly becomes a curating project. No one wants to hear everything I know on a topic—yet I still catch myself erring on the side of giving my audiences too much. I know better, but it's tough. What helps me is reframing my content for a one-hour Zoom presentation as an overview: one main thesis, three key points. Boiling down everything to those clean, essential ideas is often the hardest part.

Here's my favorite not-so-secret weapon: generative AI. I love playing with tools like ChatGPT and Perplexity to do a brain dump, distill my ideas, and make them interesting to my audience. The more context and detail I share with AI, the better the output. It's like having a brainstorming partner who never gets tired of my questions (and couldn't care less about the peanut butter pretzel crumbs on my keyboard).

Of course, I keep a skeptical eye—because AI can be like that overeager brainstorming partner who occasionally invents facts and confidently wanders off into a story about unicorns on unicycles. So, use it smartly and fact-check to keep your content real.

Why attention matters

Let's talk attention spans and retire the goldfish myth: Attention isn't a tidy 8 seconds. In real workplaces, people switch tasks often, and getting derailed is costly (Mark et al., 2015). On average, it often takes many minutes to fully get back on track after an interruption (Mark et al., 2005). We also switch frequently—one classic study found people changed activities about every three minutes (Gonzalez & Mark, 2004).

Even the best virtual presenters compete with pings, pop-ups, and pantry runs. That's why your content has to be not just good, but clear, relevant, and engaging—because your audience is always one click away from checking out. Make every second count.

Find your content's sweet spot

Let's cut to the chase. Many presenters try to cram in everything they know, instead of focusing on what their audience needs most. Before you even build your slides, ask: What does my audience care about? What do they need to remember and act on? That sweet spot—where your knowledge meets their needs—is where your best content lives.

Start strong with a story

Stories work. Start where the action is. Use specific characters, stakes, a problem to solve, and a swift resolution to hook your listener. Compared with plain facts and other non-story formats, a well-told narrative can nudge what people believe, feel, plan, and do (Braddock & Dillard, 2016). Why? When we're "transported"—pulled into the story—we're more likely to adopt story-consistent beliefs (Green & Brock, 2000).

In business, storytelling works by creating emotional resonance and helping audiences see themselves in the narrative. For example, brands like Apple master this strategy by weaving stories of creativity and innovation that invite customers to see themselves as part of a bold, cutting-edge community, not just buyers of tech products.

Simon Sinek's TED Talk, "Start with Why," is a strong example. He uses simple stories and a clear purpose to inspire leaders and organizations, even around complex topics like leadership philosophy (Sinek, 2009).

Storytelling helps audiences move beyond facts to feel motivated and connected. Yes, tell your stories extra-tight online: shorter set-ups, fewer moving parts, and clearer stakes.

A tale of two presenters

🚫 Presenter A: The content dumper

You start your presentation with a slide crammed with dense text and complex graphics, determined to share every detail of your six-month project in 30 minutes. Within seconds, half the audience is skimming their texts, and the other half is mentally plotting their escape.

✅ Presenter B: The clarity champion

You face the same mountain of data. Instead of tossing out a salad of numbers, you start with a crisp chart—a line graph highlighting the single most important trend. The chart is clear, labeled, and the message is memorable: "Here's the shift that changed everything." Your slides are accessible, your story is focused, and your message is so clear that even the most distractible audience member perks up.

Content clarity checklist
Try these (10 minutes)

Let's say you're giving a 10-minute virtual presentation on how employees can avoid phishing scams.

Example: Presenting on cybersecurity basics

Start with a hook: Open with a question, stat, or anecdote that grabs attention. For example, "What's the fastest way for hackers to access your company's data? You." That line gets attention—and tees up your key message: that employee awareness is the best first line of defense.

Focus on your audience: What do they need to know? Try something like: "If you're a new employee, here's what really matters: how to spot suspicious emails, what to do if you're unsure, and how to report a potential threat."

Keep slides simple and accessible: Use large fonts, clear visuals, and an accessibility checker to ensure everyone can follow along—including people with visual and hearing disabilities, and those who aren't fluent in English. Closed captions help more than you might think, especially for non-native English speakers and people in noisy or shared spaces. Make your layout clean, with three key bullet points and a screenshot of a phishing email. Choose a 28+ point font and use Microsoft's built-in tool to check for visual accessibility.

Use AI tools: AI can help simulate your audience's perspective. Ask ChatGPT to play a skeptical employee: "What would I want to know if hearing this for the first time?" Or use Perplexity to gather fresh examples of recent phishing scams in your industry. Other tools like Claude or Gemini can also help you explore alternative angles or test your tone. Just remember, AI sometimes hallucinates information—so double-check your facts before using them live.

Practice your story: Rehearse your delivery out loud with a colleague or into Zoom's record function. Aim for a clear, conversational tone. If it sounds robotic or over-rehearsed, practice loosening it up until it flows naturally. Or give a brain dump to a tool like NotebookLM which can turn your notes into a podcast-style summary you can listen to. That might spark new ideas or help you hear where your story needs work.

🖥️ Rookie mistakes—DON'T:

- Overload with facts; DO prioritize clarity over quantity.

- Ignore your audience's needs; DO speak to what matters most to them.

- Skip accessibility; DO make sure your content is readable and understandable for everyone including those with visual, auditory, and language-processing needs.

- Skip practice; DO rehearse like a pro.

🎬 In-person presentation strategies

Over the decades I've presented in person, I've learned that compelling content isn't just about what you say—it's about creating moments that make your audience lean in and remember. I rarely share my slides in advance and generally prefer not to distribute them afterward either, unless a client specifically asks. While some conferences still hand out bound folders packed with slides and handouts, in my world, those days are fading as I keep paper materials to a minimum to reduce waste and keep attention focused where it belongs: on the experience itself.

I'm passionate about mixing in interactive tools—whiteboards, flip charts, and even props—to break up slide decks and invite participation. I also show videos, play music, or include other media whenever it serves the content and keeps things interesting. One favorite technique is the "fortune cookie" style tips that participants pick and read aloud or write themselves for others to share; these little touches help anchor key ideas in memorable ways.

With the rise of generative AI, I've embraced live demos—showing audiences how to use AI as a powerful tool for crafting work documents, job search materials, and more. Live demos require flexibility and a willingness to be imperfect, but they create shared discovery and real connection around your content. I also like to gamify learning sometimes—for example, I use Jeopardy!-style games to test knowledge of key subjects with my NYU grad students, mixing fun and learning to keep energy high.

When your audience doesn't know each other well, I prefer tent cards or other types of name tags—clip-ons or lanyards—because sticky ones often wander off in distracting ways. These small thoughtful details help your content land more effectively in the real world.

Facilitating online meetings

Facilitating online meetings means designing content that speaks to many learning styles all at once. I keep this top of mind by using visuals (slides, shared docs), audio cues (tone, clear instructions), and active participation tools (polls, breakout rooms) to engage as many senses as possible.

A major content asset in online sessions is the chat box. Over years of virtual facilitation, I've seen the chat transform into a rich source of questions and insights that can deepen the content experience. Having a wingperson monitor it, or making space to integrate chat comments, helps keep your content responsive and interactive.

Spontaneity also adds richness to your content: If someone drops a mention of a new tool or idea, I often pivot to explore it on the spot, inviting others to experiment alongside me. This fluid, real-time discovery makes the content more dynamic and memorable.

Tech tools

You don't need fancy software to craft compelling content. But the right tools can help spark ideas, organize your thoughts, and bring your message to life. When I'm getting started, I often draft my content in Word or Google Docs—just to get the bones down. Once the structure starts to take shape, I'm happy to get into editing mode.

If you're more visual, try a virtual mind-mapping tool like Whimsical or Miro to lay out your ideas. Disclaimer: I've dabbled with tools like these but don't use them often. They're right for some folks, but I often find the setup, learning curve, and tool fatigue outweigh the payoff. Prefer low-tech? You can't beat sticky notes on a big piece of construction paper.

While I love noodling with AI tools for ideation and refinement, sometimes unplugging helps me get into a deeper flow. I go for a brisk walk or take a shower to let ideas percolate. Remember: The tools you use should make your process easier, not hijack it.

Introvert insights

As an introvert, I love the solo focus of content creation—but that butts heads with my perfectionism, aka analysis paralysis. So, I also thrive when I have a sounding board or thinking partner. Sometimes, that's a trusted colleague. Other times, it's an AI tool that helps me clarify my message without the pressure of performing or fear of judgment (since AI can live up to its reputation as a total kiss-up).

I bounce between deep-dive-alone mode and bursts of collaboration. You do you. This book's foundation is all about helping you to understand your preferences and work with them—not against them.

Just remember that drafting and editing are different stages. You don't need to get it perfect on the first pass. I lose sight of that sometimes, too. When perfectionism sneaks in wearing a "just-one-more tweak" disguise, I've gotten better(ish) at catching it early and moving on. In content creation, progress beats polish!

Picture this: Turn content into connection

It's 9:55 a.m., and your Zoom waiting room counter ticks up—13... 17... 22 people. Your desk is littered with Post-its and half-drunk coffee cups from yesterday's marathon prep session. But today, instead of frantically shuffling through tabs, your slides are loaded, focused, and ready: one main message, three crisp points, and a story to hook them from slide one.

You take a breath and click "Admit all." Smiling faces pop onto the screen. You lead with a quick, vivid story about a real customer problem—short enough to intrigue, clear enough for everyone to get it. Then you reveal a single, clean chart that nails your point. The chat lights up with "So true" and "Love this visual." By the 10-minute mark, you're not wondering if they're multitasking—you can tell from their nods and reactions that they're right there with you.

By the final slide, you've given them exactly what they need—no fluff, no overwhelm. Your closing line lands, and when you open for Q&A, the first comment seals it: "That was the clearest explanation I've heard all year."

That's the power of building your content around your audience's needs and trimming the rest.

Pro tips

- **Test your visuals for accessibility:** Use built-in checkers to ensure your slides are readable for people with visual impairments—and enable closed captions or transcripts to include those with hearing or language processing needs.

- **Ask for feedback:** Share your draft with a colleague or use AI to get suggestions for improvement.

- **Tell a story:** Even data can be memorable when you wrap it in a story.

If you're wondering how to put all this into practice, here's what works for me: When I'm stuck, I'll paste my outline or even a messy brain dump into AI like ChatGPT and ask for help distilling it into a main message and three key points. Sometimes, the AI's questions or summaries help me see what really matters to my audience (which I describe in my prompts)—and what I can leave out. If you haven't tried this yet, give it a shot. You might be surprised at how much clarity you gain, and how much you can trim without losing impact.

💡 The big idea

You don't need perfect slides, you need a message that lands. Make every moment count, focus on what matters to your audience, and use every tool (including AI, if that's your jam!) to help your story stick. But how do you know what matters to them? Whenever possible, I simply ask. That could mean reaching out to the event host, running a quick pre-event poll, or even weaving in a few targeted questions or polls into the live chat to see what hits.

Think of your content like a Venn diagram: One circle is what you want to say. The other is what your audience cares about. Aim for the overlap—and trim the rest.

Next up—Chapter 4: Let Your Voice Carry and Connect Online

In the next chapter, we'll explore how to harness your natural voice to engage virtual audiences, project confidence, and ensure your message resonates—whether you're presenting to a packed Zoom room or leading a small online meeting.

References

Braddock, K., & Dillard, J. P. (2016). Meta-analytic evidence for the persuasive effect of narratives on beliefs, attitudes, intentions, and behaviors. *Communication Monographs*, 83(4), 446–467.

Green, M. C., & Brock, T. C. (2000). The role of transportation in the persuasiveness of public narratives. *Journal of Personality and Social Psychology*, 79(5), 701–721.

Gonzalez, V. M., & Mark, G. (2004). "Constant, constant, multi-tasking craziness": Managing multiple working spheres. *Proceedings of the SIGCHI Conference on Human Factors in Computing Systems (CHI '04)*, 113–120.

Mark, G., Iqbal, S. T., Czerwinski, M., & Johns, P. (2015). Focused, aroused, but so distractible: A temporal perspective on multitasking and communications. *Proceedings of the 18th ACM Conference on Computer Supported Cooperative Work & Social Computing (CSCW '15)*, 903–916.

Mark, G., Gonzalez, V. M., & Harris, J. (2005). No task left behind? Examining the nature of fragmented work. *Proceedings of the SIGCHI Conference on Human Factors in Computing Systems (CHI '05)*, 321–330.

Sinek, S. (2009, September). How great leaders inspire action [Video]. TED Conferences.

Chapter 4

Let Your Voice Carry and Connect Online

In the three-legged stool of effective online presentations—content, voice, and body language—we just covered the crucial role of content in the previous chapter. Now, it's time to focus on the second leg, voice. It is one of your most powerful tools to keep your audience engaged and connected, especially when body language cues are limited in virtual settings. Mastering your vocal delivery strengthens the stool and elevates your entire presentation.

You're in the middle of delivering a virtual presentation. Your words, once conversational, now fade like a WiFi signal clinging to a single bar. As you speak, telltale signs of disconnection appear: Chat messages and applause emojis fizzle, and fewer heads nod in agreement. The energy in your virtual space is evaporating—quietly but completely—and with it, your confidence.

Unlike with in-person settings, there's no dramatic audience exit—just fewer and fewer squares on your screen—and maybe you spot this left behind in chat: "Thanks, this was great. Running to my next meeting." When the energy wanes and the audience is ducking out, it's your job to step it up. Robotic "presenting" is a death knell. You need a more animated, tuned in version of you. The medium itself—tiny squares and tinny mics, tamps down energy. So, it's up to you to add dimension.

Why your voice matters

Voice is one of the most powerful and most overlooked tools in virtual communication. It's a key bridge between your content and your audience's attention. A resonant, varied voice signals confidence and investment in your message and keeps people listening. When your delivery sounds monotone, tense, flat, rushed, forced into a pitch that's higher or lower than natural, it can be harder for your message to land.

Evidence backs this up: Research shows that listeners find speakers with cues such as varied tone, rhythm, and repeated phrases more compelling and credible (Rosenberg & Hirschberg, 2009). These vocal patterns are some of the key ways speakers come across as charismatic. The classic Crazy Eddie commercials from my New York childhood come to mind: "With prices so low, they're practically giving it away," delivered with that zingy, animated voice that still sticks in my head.

Persuasion studies go further: Subtle shifts in intonation, pitch, and speech rate shape how confident listeners perceive a speaker to be (Guyer et al., 2019). Related research shows that when speakers vary their loudness and modulation, those cues also signal confidence—and that perception of confidence makes them more persuasive (Van Zant & Berger, 2020).

Now that you know why your voice matters, here's how to put that knowledge into practice. If your voice gets in the way of being heard, you have options. Start with a public speaking class or Toastmasters International meeting, go further with a voice coach, and if you suspect a speech or fluency disorder, consider reaching out to a licensed speech-language pathologist.

Voice bias is real—but you have options

Bias against higher-pitched voices, particularly associated with women, is real and unfair. In controlled experiments, female and male listeners alike tended to prefer lower-pitched voices—even when evaluating female political candidates—illustrating a bias to notice but not obey (Klofstad, Anderson, & Peters, 2012). The point isn't to change your pitch; it's to use variety, pacing, and emphasis so your message carries despite the bias.

My aim in this chapter isn't to change how you sound, but to help you understand how your delivery affects your audience, and to give you specific vocal techniques to engage your listeners.

What it sounds like when you're grounded

When I'm at my best, I sound like I'm immersed in a conversation with my audience, even when I'm doing most of the talking. My voice is relaxed, my pace intentional, my tone responsive. But when nerves hit, I can slip into my kindergarten teacher voice, higher pitched with an overly cheerful tone. I've learned to hear when that happens and adjust on the fly by slowing down, pausing for breath, and emphasizing my key ideas. I have come to know what my grounded voice sounds like and can easily return to it when I notice that I have gone astray. What gets your voice grounded?

Coming from a vocally grounded place is especially crucial online. Video conferencing increases cognitive load, making attention more fragile than in person (Bailenson, 2021). Your voice can flatten or drift more online, so it has to do extra work to keep people with you. That's why your vocal delivery matters: It's how your presence travels and your message sticks.

Clear pacing, natural inflection, and thoughtful emphasis connect you to your audience and get your point across. Clarity, variety, and emphasis can make your voice sound compelling and can draw your listeners in, far more than some imaginary "perfect" speaker voice ever could.

When nerves hijack your voice—and how to get it back

Many presenters default to a personality-free delivery when under pressure. That's because nerves can trigger your body's stress response—cue shallow breathing, tight vocal cords, and sudden shifts in pitch. When you're under stress, intrinsic laryngeal muscles in your throat become more activated, which can lead to pitch shifts and a strained or jumpy voice (Helou et al., 2018). Research consistently shows that emotion changes how the voice sounds: shifts in pitch, loudness, and timing (Scherer, 2003).

Noticing these physical cues is the first step. Once you do, you can begin making conscious vocal choices—like slowing your pace, softening your tone, or adding emphasis—to help your delivery feel more grounded and engaging.

When I work with clients, I ask them to tell me about something they love—traveling, running, cooking—and I gently ask them questions until they forget they're "performing." That's often when their natural voice emerges: a warm tone, authentic rhythm, and animated pacing. Sometimes we even record the conversation so they can hear how natural and resonant their voice sounds when they're at ease.

If your nerves take over when you present online, you're not alone. Chapter 2, "Manage Jitters," offers strategies to keep your cool when anxiety creeps in. Here, we're focusing on how to get the most from your voice—how to keep it expressive and true to you.

Getting more comfortable with your voice

Before we dive into exercises, let's talk about getting more comfortable with your voice. Many people cringe when they hear recordings of themselves speaking. Add video to the mix and it's even more jarring. That reaction is common and doesn't mean anything's wrong with you. In fact, there's science behind it.

Normally, you hear yourself in two ways: through the air and through vibrations in your skull. Those vibrations add depth, so your voice sounds lower to you than to others. Recordings capture only the sound through the air, which is why playback often sounds thinner or higher (Reinfeldt et al., 2010). As a child, I enjoyed talking through a paper towel tube, making my voice boomier (the opposite of what happens with a recording). Either way, the version you hear doesn't quite match the one everyone else hears.

Build your comfort level, one recording at a time

Social anxiety can amplify your discomfort with your voice. Research shows that those with higher social anxiety not only tend to dislike their recorded voice but may even fail to recognize it, reflecting their heightened self-consciousness (Jogia et al., 2024).

Many of my grad students—especially those who speak English as an additional language—tell me they feel self-conscious about their accents or word choices, even though they're fluent. That discomfort can be a barrier to feeling confident. If that rings true for you, remember this: Your voice deserves to be heard.

Like anything that you wish to get better at, the more you practice, the more conversational you'll become. Listen to your voice recordings with a constructive mindset. Start with low-pressure practice: read a favorite short story or article aloud—it's less pressure than rehearsing your own presentation yet still gives you helpful insights.

Some clients say the voice they hear on playback sounds unfamiliar. That's normal. With repetition, the jarring sensation often fades, and familiarity breeds comfort.

Ditching the illusion of the perfect voice

Many assume they must meet a mythical speaker standard: polished, powerful, perfect. You don't need to be a voice-over artist to be impactful in your online presentation. It's okay if your voice quivers, your pitch jumps, or you stumble over a word. You don't need to sound flawless; you just need to sound worth listening to. That starts with sounding like yourself.

Jumpstart your voice

Try vocal warmups before your next presentation. Tongue twisters wake up your articulation and help you loosen up without overthinking. A few to try:

- "Red leather, yellow leather"
- "Unique New York"
- "Sally sells seashells by the seashore"

Forget speed. Aim for clarity and playfulness.

A tale of two presenters

🚫 Presenter A: The monotone yammerer

As you speak, you notice your voice echoing through your own empty, gray hallway. Each syllable thuds like a footstep. Your message is falling flat. Your audience's blank expressions indicate that if asked to summarize your talk, they'd likely just recall a foggy blur. Your audience drifts—some nodding like dashboard dogs, others fading, still others visibly straining to stay engaged. You suspect some are glancing at their text messages with their camera off, hoping their disengagement will go unnoticed.

 Presenter B: The voice virtuoso

You orchestrate your voice like a conductor, emphasizing key points with strategic pauses and varied volume. You speak with natural enthusiasm and minimal filler words, and your pitch rises and falls to keep attention. When you pause before key points, the audience leans in slightly, anticipating what comes next.

Vocal workout and challenge solutions
Try these (50 minutes)

Volume check (5 minutes)

> **Challenge:** Speaking too softly.
>
> **Solution:** Practice projecting from your diaphragm, not your throat (or nose).
>
> **Quick fix:** Breathe consciously and use an external microphone positioned a few inches from your mouth.
>
> **Exercise:** Record yourself presenting the same sentence three ways: too soft (as if whispering a secret across a crowded room), too loud (as if shouting at someone standing right next to you), and just right (as if speaking to a friend across a small table in a quiet café). Listen for which recorded sounds are most natural and engaging.

Pacing/Pauses (5 minutes)

Challenge: Racing through content or speaking at a constant pace without pauses.

Solution: Mark pauses in your notes with // symbols or color-coding; I just use the word "PAUSE" in big red letters.

Quick fix: Take three deep breaths before starting and try a metronome app to maintain a steady pace.

Exercise: Practice varying your speed—from deliberately slow (as if reading a long list of terms as slowly as possible) to conversationally brisk. Add strategic pauses before key points, treating them as verbal punctuation marks (as if telling a dramatic story, pausing for effect before revealing a key detail).

Tone/Emotion (10 minutes)

Challenge: Sounding unmodulated, disengaged, or lacking appropriate emotion for the context.

Solution: Connect with the meaning of your words and let your emotions naturally color your voice.

Quick fix: Think of your presentation as a conversation with a friend on a topic you're passionate about.

Exercise: Record yourself telling a story you love. Hear the natural variation in your tone and the emotions you express. Identify a section of your presentation where you want to convey a specific emotion (e.g., excitement, concern, curiosity). Record yourself presenting that section multiple times, each time focusing on expressing the desired emotion through your tone.

Pitch (5 minutes)

Challenge: Sounding forced and straining your vocal cords by deepening your voice or speaking in an unnaturally high pitch.

Solution: Allow your pitch to vary naturally, as you would in a relaxed conversation.

Quick fix: Think of your content as a conversation with a friend.

Exercise: Record yourself telling a story about something you love—notice how your pitch naturally varies when you're excited about your topic. Now bring that same energy to your presentation content.

"Upspeak" (Minimal instances) (5 minutes)

Challenge: Making statements sound like questions (often unconsciously).

Solution: Practice ending sentences with a downward inflection.

Quick fix: Visualize a period at the end of each statement, rather than a question mark. Recent experiments show that ending sentences with a downward tone (rather than an upward one) makes speakers sound more confident and influential (Vaughan-Johnston et al., 2024).

Exercise: Record yourself making statements. If your voice rises at the end, practice keeping it level or dropping slightly downward.

Emphasis on keywords (5 minutes)

Challenge: Failing to highlight important words or phrases

Solution: Use slight changes in volume, pitch, or pace to emphasize keywords.

Quick fix: Underline or highlight keywords in your notes as a reminder.

Exercise: Select a paragraph from your presentation. Identify the keywords that you think would resonate most with your audience. Record yourself reading the paragraph, experimenting with different ways to emphasize those keywords (e.g., pausing briefly before them, saying them slightly louder or slower, varying your pitch momentarily for emphasis).

Sentence length (varied) (5 minutes)

Challenge: Using sentences that are all the same length, which can sound dull.

Solution: Vary your sentence length to create a more dynamic and engaging rhythm.

Quick fix: Read your presentation out loud and listen for sections that sound choppy or plodding. Experiment with breaking up long sentences or combining short ones.

Exercise: Rewrite a section of your presentation, intentionally varying the length of your sentences. Record yourself reading both the original and the revised versions. Compare how they sound.

Enunciation (5 minutes)

Challenge: Mumbling or rushing words together.

Solution: Practice over-enunciating during rehearsals.

Quick fix: Imagine each word as a distinct pearl on a string.

Exercise: Record yourself reading a paragraph, first as if with a mouthful of mashed potatoes, then with exaggerated enunciation (like a news reporter emphasizing each syllable for maximum clarity). Finally, find the sweet spot to sound crisp and natural.

Avoiding filler (5 minutes)

Challenge: Overusing filler words such as "um," "uh," "like," and "you know."

Solution: Practice pausing silently instead of using filler, and slow down to support that process.

Quick fix: Use a timer and try speaking for increasing intervals without any filler.

Exercise: Record yourself presenting a section of your presentation. Count the number of fillers you use. Repeat the exercise, consciously trying to replace fillers with pauses.

🖥 Rookie mistakes—DON'T:

- Put up with subpar sound quality; DO invest in a high-quality mic or at least use a headset, and remember to do a sound check.

- Let your volume trail off at the ends of sentences—your words shouldn't vanish like steam at a subway grate; DO project your voice throughout.

- Speak in a monotone (aka a sleep soundtrack); DO read your content aloud and ask, Would low-attention audience members stay awake through this?

- Rush through key points without breath or emphasis; DO give ideas time to land.

- Skip practice (yes, your audience can tell); DO discover the amount of rehearsal you need to perform at your best.

- Forget to breathe or hydrate before you speak; DO treat your voice like an instrument—give it the air and water it needs.

These are common pitfalls, but you've already seen how to sidestep them with the strategies we've covered so far. Up next, let's cover a few in-person presentation tips, where tech and room dynamics are essentials in shaping your delivery.

🎬 In-person presentation strategies

While the tips and techniques we've covered apply everywhere, in-person venues bring distinct vocal needs. Don't forget to adjust your volume for the room size—project your voice naturally if you're not using a mic; if you are, always test it first. Some mics require you to hold them at a certain angle to be heard, while others (like lavalier mics) let you set 'em and forget 'em. Just remember to turn them off during bathroom trips and private conversations during breaks! Personally, I prefer a lavalier mic because I like to use gestures when I speak, and I find it challenging to remember to keep a handheld mic close to my mouth.

Facilitating online meetings

Voice-centric tips:

- **Use vocal cues to guide participation:** Signal when it's someone else's turn to speak by pausing, lowering your volume, or using an inviting intonation ("Would anyone like to add?").

- **Project warmth and clarity:** Greet participants by name and use a friendly tone to set a welcoming atmosphere, helping everyone feel included.

- **Vary your pace and emphasis:** Slow down when introducing new topics or summarizing action items and use vocal emphasis to highlight key points.

- **Invite quieter voices:** Use gentle prompts ("I'd love to hear from someone who hasn't spoken yet").

- **Normalize pauses:** Let your voice signal that silence is intentional and valuable, giving participants time to think before responding.

- **Summarize with vocal energy:** At the end of a discussion, recap decisions or next steps with a clear, confident delivery to reinforce understanding and keep momentum.

Tech tools

- **Voice recording apps for practice** (e.g., Voice Memos for recording and playback on Apple devices; Audacity, a free, open-source audio editor for more advanced editing).

- **Pitch monitoring apps to check vocal variety** (e.g., Vocular, which provides real-time pitch feedback; Singscope, which analyzes pitch accuracy and variation).

- **Timer apps to practice pacing** (e.g., Toastmasters Timer, specifically designed for timing speeches, Presenter Timer, a simple timer with customizable intervals).

- **Audio enhancement tools to improve sound quality** (e.g., Krisp for noise cancellation; Nvidia Broadcast for noise removal and audio effects using AI).

Introvert insights

As an introvert who's guided many others, I know many of us speak softly—especially when we're nervous. But repeated practice and self-recording reveal your vocal strengths. Many of my introvert clients speak softly but nail emphasis, pauses, and enunciation, quiet strengths that project powerful presence.

Picture this: Speaking so they lean in, not tune out

It's 11:59 a.m., and you've already run through your slides twice this morning. But when you click "Start meeting," your heart still sprints. You hear yourself launching into the opener—only to notice your pitch creeping higher and faster, like you've downed too much coffee.

You pause, breathe, and drop your shoulders. This time your words land at your natural pitch, steadier. You stretch out the next phrase, giving it space. A hint of warmth sneaks back into your tone. Heads start nodding. The chat lights up with " 👏 " emojis. You're no longer pushing sound out—you're in a conversation.

That's the power of a grounded, varied voice. It carries confidence, signals presence, sounds persuasive, and pulls your audience toward you—even through those tiny squares.

Pro tip

Everyone has their own vocal style, strengths, and challenges, but certain techniques consistently help virtual presenters engage their listeners. Start by recording yourself talking about something you love, then apply that same vocal energy to your presentations. Because energy can flatten on a screen, and that includes the energy of your voice, remember to dial it up online.

💡 The big idea

Your voice is a powerful instrument. Research shows that a monotone voice is a charisma killer, especially in virtual meetings where other body cues are minimal. When speakers vary volume, pitch, and pacing—even slightly—listeners judge them as more confident and are more likely to be persuaded. In virtual settings, your voice does double duty—it carries not just your message, but your presence. Your voice shapes rhythm, highlights key ideas, and keeps your audience with you. Practice, replay, refine. The more you tune this instrument, the stronger it becomes.

Next up—Chapter 5: Sharpen Your Body Language and Eye Contact

In the next chapter, we'll explore how to support your message with body language and eye contact to complement your best voice for a compelling online presentation.

References

Bailenson, J. N. (2021). Nonverbal overload: A theoretical argument for the causes of Zoom fatigue. *Technology, Mind, and Behavior*, 2(1).

Guyer, J. J., Fabrigar, L. R., & Vaughan-Johnston, T. I. (2019). Speech rate, intonation, and pitch: Investigating the bias and cue effects of vocal confidence on persuasion. *Personality and Social Psychology Bulletin*, 45(3), 389-405.

Helou, L. B., Rosen, C. A., Wang, W., & Verdolini Abbott, K. (2018). Intrinsic laryngeal muscle response to a public speech preparation stressor. *Journal of Speech, Language, and Hearing Research*, 61(7), 1525–1543.

Jogia, J., Thomas, J., Barbato, M., & Bentall, R. (2024). Social anxiety, voice confrontation and voice recognition: A bilingual exploration. *International Journal of Psychology*, 59(6), 1084–1090.

Klofstad, C. A., Anderson, R. C., & Peters, S. (2012). Sounds like a winner: Voice pitch influences perception of leadership capacity. *Proceedings of the Royal Society B: Biological Sciences*, 279(1738), 2698–2704.

Reinfeldt, S., Östli, P., Håkansson, B., & Stenfelt, S. (2010). Hearing one's own voice during phoneme vocalization—Transmission by air and bone conduction. *Journal of the Acoustical Society of America*, 128(2), 751–762.

Rosenberg, A., & Hirschberg, J. (2009). Charisma perception from speech and text. Speech

Scherer, K. R. (2003). Vocal communication of emotion: A review of research paradigms. *Speech Communication*, 40(1–2), 227–256.

Van Zant, A. B., & Berger, J. (2020). How the voice persuades. *Journal of Personality and Social Psychology*, 118(4), 661–682.

Vaughan-Johnston, T. I., Leder, S., & Ball, T. (2024). Intonation and influence: How sentence endings shape perceptions of confidence. *Journal of Experimental Social Psychology*, 108, 104500.

Chapter 5

Sharpen Your Body Language and Eye Contact

For online presentations, including meetings and job interviews, a strong delivery rests on three legs, like a sturdy stool: content, voice, and body language. In the prior two chapters, we covered the first two, crafting strong content and bringing out your best voice. Now let's get to work on body language.

Body language: The third leg of your delivery

This chapter focuses on sharpening your body language and "eye contact" with the camera because if they are weak, your message can lose its impact. Think of tech, lighting, and background as the floor beneath your stool, providing essential support. Meanwhile, the three legs of the stool—strong content, vocal variety, and sharp body language—bear the main weight of your presentation.

The power of nonverbal communication

Nonverbal communication is crucial in person and online. For example, in recorded talks, Van Edwards finds that top-rated TED speakers use nearly twice as many hand gestures as less engaging ones; gestures were directly associated with higher audience ratings (Van Edwards, 2017; Rodero, 2022). I believe in finding a rhythm that's expressive but not exaggerated—somewhere between an orchestra conductor and a statue.

Effective online body language uses your entire upper body to reinforce your message. Your content and vocal tone set the stage, but your onscreen presence shapes the energy in the "room." Rodero (2022) also shows that moderate hand gestures and varied vocal pitch (not just volume) make speakers appear more effective and engaging.

When I first began presenting online, I was acutely aware of every imperfection—the glare from my glasses, the uncertainty of where to look. Focusing on one skill at a time—eye contact, then gestures, then posture—not only grounded me physically but made good habits automatic. I now help clients approach nonverbal skills in that same sequence: master eye contact, then add gestures, then posture. For in-person presentations, we include elements like purposeful walking and standing still. Each layer becomes muscle memory: automatic, freeing, and effective.

The emotional reality of online presenting

If you are anything like me, presenting online makes you feel vulnerable. Seeing yourself in the video feed, it's natural to notice every detail: lighting, framing, posture, gestures, eye contact. When you are distracted by a crooked collar or lipstick on your teeth, or if you are critical of your looks in general, you lose your audience's attention. Sharpening your body language and eye contact will shift you away from your hall of mirrors and back toward your audience.

A client of mine, a senior financial analyst, came to me convinced she just wasn't "a camera person." In our first session, her shoulders were tense, her arms barely moved, and she spoke in a monotone. Together, we focused on just one thing: posture. She practiced sitting back so her shoulders were visible and relaxed, and the change was instant—her voice gained energy, resonance, and clarity and she looked more at ease.

The following week, we added simple gestures to reinforce key points. By the third session, she was smiling into the camera as naturally as she did in person. Her transformation wasn't about becoming someone else; it was about unlocking a version of herself she already knew in person and learning to let it show on screen. Her success reflects the gradual layering I encourage; start with one nonverbal skill, then add the next, until it feels natural.

When the audience seems far away

Have you ever prepared thoroughly, only to find yourself presenting to a sea of blank screens or faces looking elsewhere? Even with compelling content, something feels off. So often, it's not what you say in that little box, but how your presence fills the frame that makes the biggest difference in connecting.

This is an opportunity to show your online personality and presence, from head to shoulders. When you fill that frame, you create a sense of intimacy and focus—making you harder to ignore and helping build a stronger bond with your audience. A well-filled frame lets your expressions and gestures come through vividly, turning a distant screen into a personal encounter.

Finding your flow

Every online audience is different; discovering your flow together matters. Observing audience cues helps you decide when to move forward, pause, or adjust your pace. Research shows that nonverbal cues can rival spoken words in shaping interactions (Bonaccio, et al.).

Recent studies in telemedicine and video conferencing further highlight the vital role of facial expressions, eye contact, and body language in building empathy and social presence through screens (Rahmanti et al., 2025; Helou et al., 2022; Shinya et al., 2024). Online, the challenge intensifies: You must project presence, hold attention, and use body language—especially eye contact with the camera—to sustain connection, even when it feels just out of reach.

A tale of two presenters

🚫 Presenter A: The statue

You start your video and just sit there, arms pinned to your sides. Your eyes bounce between your notes and the camera, rarely giving the sense of true eye contact. You might as well be a mannequin on mute. The audience's attention drifts; your presence, static as a screensaver, isn't reaching anyone.

✓ Presenter B: The engaged communicator

You use open, welcoming gestures that stay in frame and feel purposeful. You lean in a bit. Genuine interest radiates from the screen. Your eyes meet the camera. A smile breaks through and the whole room, virtual as it is, feels warmer. No need to be a charisma machine—just inviting, present, and real. Aim for energy that feels like the best version of you rather than a character you're playing. Forced enthusiasm can be as off-putting as too little.

The difference between these two presenters often comes down to a few intentional shifts. The following approaches will help you make them second nature.

Body language and eye contact challenge
Try these (40 minutes)

Practice is the key to your progress; awareness alone won't shape your onscreen presence. Below are four focus areas; record yourself to get a clear, objective view of what's working and what to refine.

Framing and posture (10 minutes)

Challenge: Sitting too close, too far, or slouching.

Solution: Frame your upper body (head and shoulders) so your gestures are fully visible and your presence feels at ease.

Quick fix: Prop your camera at eye level, even with a stack of books. Sit far enough back to include your head and shoulders so your gestures stay fully visible. Find your sweet spot: close enough to connect, far enough to avoid overwhelming your audience.

Exercise: Record yourself at different camera heights and distances. Watch for the point where you appear relaxed—close enough to feel personable and far enough to avoid looming. That balance is your sweet spot.

Hand and arm gestures (10 minutes)

Challenge: Distracting or invisible gestures.

Solution: If you use hand or arm gestures, make them fully visible and purposeful—inside your video frame. Deliberate, open gestures reinforce your message.

Quick fix: For built-in cameras, imagine a "gesture zone" box on your screen. Using an external camera? Place sticky notes just outside the frame for boundaries.

Exercise: Present a short segment with gestures, then without. Compare the recordings. Do your gestures support your message or distract from it?

Eye contact (10 minutes)

Challenge: Looking down at notes instead of the camera.

Solution: Look into the camera to create the impression of direct eye contact; this makes each participant feel addressed.

Quick fix: Place a tiny sticker or note with a smiley face on it beside your lens as a visual anchor. For a quirky little hack, affix a false eyelash right above your camera lens.

Exercise: Deliver three short messages, practicing "lens focus." Increase the length of time you look into the lens to build comfort while still glancing occasionally at participants' faces to gauge reactions.

Facial expressions (10 minutes)

Challenge: A neutral or disengaged expression.

Solution: Aim for facial expressions that feel honest and just a touch more expressive than in everyday conversation to counteract the flattening effect of the screen.

Quick fix: Picture explaining something you care about to a trusted colleague. Let genuine enthusiasm, concern, or interest show through a smile or raised eyebrows.

Exercise: Record a segment using different expressions. Aim for authenticity and resonance, not a game-show host grin.

💻 Rookie mistakes—DON'T:

- Let your body language contradict your message; DO reinforce your words with matching gestures, voice, and facial expressions.

- Ignore cultural differences in nonverbal cues; DO learn about your audience's norms and adapt accordingly.

- Fidget, slump, or let a cranky expression creep in; DO hold a grounded, open posture and project presence intentionally.

The personal style factor

All your life, you've used your body to communicate, but online presenting requires an extra layer of intentionality. There's no single formula—it's part skill, part personal style. Some presenters are classic and steady, like Aretha Franklin; others are dynamic and edgy, like Prince. Some glide like ballroom dancers; others bring the charge of a mosh pit. The goal isn't to change who you are—it's to bring out your best professional self while keeping your audience's needs front and center.

🎬 In-person presentation strategies

- Make eye contact with individuals in different parts of the room for about three seconds each. As you do, turn your shoulders directly toward each person to show genuine connection.

- Use your full body for energetic delivery

- Stand still on purpose; move with intention

- Walk deliberately to re-engage your audience

Dancing with hybrid and hy-flex challenges

The first time I was really put to the test with hybrid and hy-flex presentations was over a dozen years ago at a Manhattan hedge fund. I was giving a presentation—on presentation skills!—to a live audience while a robot on wheels rolled around the room, beaming me simultaneously to remote viewers. I did my darndest to "dance with the robot," squaring my shoulders to match its angle, planting my feet firmly to stay grounded, and locking eyes with it for three seconds at a time, just as I did with anyone in the room. It was like trying to cha-cha with a disco ball on wheels—sometimes tricky to keep in sync but essential to making both my 3D in-person audience and my 2D remote one feel like I was speaking directly to them.

What hybrid and hy-flex really mean

To unpack the jargon a bit: hybrid presentations typically offer a mix of in-person and virtual options, sometimes simultaneously, sometimes not, often with recordings for those who can't join live. Hy-flex (hybrid-flexible) takes it a step further by integrating live, equal participation for both groups at the same time, letting presenters and audiences truly connect across digital divides.

No wonder hybrid presentations keep me on my toes, and hy-flex keeps me on my tippy toes! Balancing energy, eye contact, posture, and body language across physical and virtual audiences is a challenge; but when done well, it pays off.

If you aim to include everyone, whether they're right there or watching from miles away, this dance between worlds is where your skills shine. Some days, presenting online is like competing on *Dancing with the Stars*—except you have multiple dance partners and they're beaming in from every part of the cloud. The choreography can be tricky, but when you find your groove, your whole audience, both in the room and on screen, feels the rhythm together.

Facilitating online meetings

Ground rules matter: Whenever possible, invite participants to keep cameras on for greater connection and to level the playing field. I used to dread asking for cameras on—worried it seemed invasive. But after one session where not a single face appeared, I realized faceless rectangles make it nearly impossible to read the group's mood.

Now, I frame it as a way to level the playing field: "If you're able, please turn your camera on so we can connect as humans, not just voices. If that's not possible for you, that's okay." Plan for regular short breaks when cameras and mics can be off.

Running successful online meetings means being attuned to a variety of dynamics—engaging participants across different locations, modes of attendance, and even time zones. Whether your meeting is purely virtual, hybrid, or hy-flex, the goal remains the same: to create an environment where everyone feels connected and heard.

Reading the room: Tuning in to group dynamics

Whether in person or online, be attuned to energy and flow. Cues can be subtle or delayed; learning to read the room (or screen) takes practice. Focus on monitoring participant signals—such as typing in chat, using reactions, nodding, or shifting—just like you would monitor system feedback or dashboard alerts. These signals give you real-time insight into the group's attention and mood, and research shows that the rhythm of turn-taking and conversational flow influences whether people feel included and connected. (Koudenburg, Postmes, & Gordijn, 2017).

Nonverbal cues like posture, gestures, and gaze don't just support your message—they directly shape perceptions of credibility and persuasiveness (Burgoon, Guerrero, & Floyd, 2016). What does this mean for you as a facilitator? That persuasion isn't just in the words you choose; it's in how you hold the room. A confident posture, steady gaze, and deliberate pauses can draw participants in and encourage even quiet voices to contribute. In hybrid and hy-flex formats, that becomes even more important, because you're managing energy across physical and digital spaces at once.

Tech tools

Start with what you already have—your phone camera, a mirror, or free recording software. Then add tools only if they serve your style and goals. Bailenson (2021) identifies several contributors to Zoom fatigue—excessive close-up eye gaze, constant self-view, and cognitive load, or mental strain. Practical adjustments such as posture reminders or simulated eye contact aim at those very factors and can help reduce strain.

- **Logitech Logi Tune:** Software that works with Logitech webcams to fine-tune settings like exposure and framing adjustments so you appear to look more directly at the camera. (Use only if you already have a Logitech camera; otherwise, your platform settings are usually enough.)

- **NVIDIA Broadcast (PC only):** AI-powered eye contact correction and background noise removal. Helpful if you're on Windows and want a natural gaze without staring into the screen the entire time.

- **Upright GO 2 / GO S:** A small wearable that gently vibrates to remind you to sit tall. For presenters who tend to slump, it's a discreet coaching tool.

- **Zoom, Teams, or Loom recordings:** Record yourself to review your eye contact, gestures, and posture. Most platforms now have free or low-cost record/review features built in.

- **Native backgrounds (Zoom, Teams, Meet):** Blur your real background for privacy and focus. If you use virtual backgrounds, choose professional ones and avoid clichés (I confess I'm still virtual Golden Gate Bridge'd out!).

- **Descript:** All-in-one tool for recording, editing, and reviewing video. Particularly useful if you want to transcribe, cut filler words, or analyze nonverbal patterns over time.

- **XSplit VCam:** Offers finer background blur and custom branding (like a crisp company logo). Most useful if you regularly switch between platforms; otherwise, your native background options are usually sufficient.

Introvert insights

As an introvert, I recharge through quiet reflection rather than constant interaction. That's why extended eye contact with the camera can feel draining — it mimics the intensity of being "on" with a large group, without the natural pauses you'd get in person. To manage that, I treat camera eye contact like interval training: short bursts, then rest. For me, it's a sprint, not a marathon — I lock eyes with the lens for a few sentences, then give myself a breather. Otherwise, Zoom fatigue isn't just a meme; it's my reality.

Remember that a small boost in expressiveness on camera can feel much bigger to your audience. I'm not naturally smiley (even if I'm feeling happy), but I remind myself to smile extra for the camera to warm up the "room." If seeing yourself makes you self-conscious, use your platform's "hide self-view" setting.

While introverts may need to pace their energy, extroverts often thrive on visible expressiveness. If you're naturally animated, that's an asset online—your gestures and energy can light up the screen. The key is channeling it with intention: keep movements within the camera frame and avoid letting enthusiasm spill into fidgeting. For extroverts, the challenge is usually not finding energy but focusing it so your presence feels dynamic rather than overwhelming.

Accessibility and cultural considerations

When your audience is culturally diverse, research their common body language and eye contact norms. For example, sustained eye contact may signal confidence in some cultures but be considered aggressive or disrespectful in others. Gestures like the "okay" sign may be friendly in one country and offensive in another. If you're unsure, ask a colleague from that culture, consult a cultural etiquette guide, or watch videos of local speakers presenting. When in doubt, aim for a moderate, neutral style—open gestures, pleasant facial expressions, and respectful framing—helping you avoid extremes that could unintentionally alienate parts of your audience.

Accessibility matters just as much. Ensure your visuals have text alternatives or verbal descriptions, and keep your slides high-contrast and uncluttered for those using screen readers or captions. Speak at a measured pace so captions keep up, and avoid covering your mouth when speaking so lip readers can follow. Building in these small choices creates an inclusive environment, showing you value every participant's ability to connect with your message.

Handling technical issues

Before I go "on air," I ask if someone can serve as my tech wingperson to monitor chat and flag issues so I can focus on my delivery. If you have to troubleshoot solo, slow down, breathe, and make deliberate adjustments. Calm gestures and steady tone reassure your audience.

Picture this: Own your digital stage

Imagine stepping onto your digital stage—a space both intimate and expansive, where every gesture, glance, and posture commands the attention of your scattered audience. You aren't just speaking; you're performing a dance between camera and crowd. With your upper body framed like a well-composed portrait, your movements become language, and your eyes, locked gently on the lens, send signals of confidence and connection across the virtual divide.

Picture yourself leaning in at just the right moment, hands open and steady, a genuine smile playing at the corners of your mouth. You navigate the rhythm of your presentation like a skilled dancer, aware of every subtle cue from faces on screen—nods, smiles, pauses—that tell you you're holding the room together, whether physical or virtual.

No need for flamboyance or a perfect routine. Think more of finding a groove that feels authentically you but tuned for this once-in-a-lifetime moment. With each session, those movements become a seamless extension of your message, turning a pixelated grid into a living, breathing audience.

To help maintain this connection, use practical tools, like positioning your camera at eye level and placing a small reminder near the lens to encourage simulated eye contact. These subtle adjustments enhance your sense of presence and help keep your audience with you.

That's online presence in action—the art of being so visually and energetically present that your message lands fully, no matter the distance.

Pro tip

Create a "virtual handshake"—a simple, consistent ritual at the start and end of each meeting. It might be a wave, a lean toward the camera, or a quick thumbs-up. For example, Oprah Winfrey's signature audience welcome—her warm, direct camera wave with "Are you ready?"—is a classic example. Add a few seconds of royalty-free music for extra polish.

💡 The big idea

Your style in the digital box—your posture, expressions, gestures, and eye contact—matters. It's one of three core skill sets that help your message land. Think about that three-legged stool: content, voice, and body language. Authenticity beats polish. Practice, tweak, and make your presentation your own. You may be surprised at how much more rapport you can create, even through a screen.

I often remind myself and my clients: Your expertise should be a given when you're the presenter. Body language online isn't about perfection. It's about building comfort and skill step by step. Be patient with yourself and focus on one technique at a time until it feels familiar. Each move becomes a little smoother, and each audience more of a partner in your goal— as you build your own winning rhythm of digital rapport.

Next up—Chapter 6: Prevent and Handle Technical Issues with Confidence

In the next chapter, we'll explore how to prevent and handle technical issues with confidence so you can stay composed and professional even when the unexpected happens.

References

Bailenson, J. N. (2021). Nonverbal overload: A theoretical argument for the causes of Zoom fatigue. *Technology, Mind, and Behavior*, 2(1).

Bonaccio, S., O'Reilly, J., O'Sullivan, S. L., & Chiocchio, F. (2016). Nonverbal behavior and communication in the workplace: A review and an agenda for research. *Journal of Management*, 42(5), 1044–1074.

Burgoon, J. K., Guerrero, L. K., & Floyd, K. (2016). Nonverbal communication. Routledge.

Helou, S., El Helou, E., Evans, N., Shigematsu, T., Kaneko, M., & Kiyono, K. (2022). Physician eye contact in telemedicine video consultations. *International Journal of Medical Informatics*, 165, 104825.

Koudenburg, N., Postmes, T., & Gordijn, E. H. (2017). Beyond content of conversation: The role of conversational form in the emergence and regulation of social structure. *Personality and Social Psychology Review*, 21(1), 50–71.

Rahmanti, A. R., Yang, H.-C., Huang, C.-W., Huang, C.-T., Lazuardi, L., Lin, C.-W., & Li, Y.-C. J. (2025). Validating nonverbal cues for assessing physician empathy in telemedicine: A Delphi study. *Medical Education Online*, 30(1), 2497328.

Rodero, E. (2022). Effectiveness, attractiveness, and emotional response to voice pitch and hand gestures in public speaking. *Frontiers in Communication*, 7, 869084.

Shinya, M., Yamane, N., Mori, Y., & Teaman, B. (2024). Off-camera gaze decreases evaluation scores in a simulated online job interview. *Scientific Reports*, 14, 12056.

Van Edwards, V. (2017, March 1). The surprising power of body language in TED speakers. *Toastmasters Magazine*.

Chapter 6

Prevent and Handle
Technical Issues with Confidence

In virtual presenting, technical hiccups aren't an "if"—they're a "when." Every presenter faces them; I do, too. Technical breakdowns used to shake my confidence: I'd panic-click, over-apologize, and imagine my credibility evaporating in real time. One day everything failed at once, and I realized I needed a better playbook. In the end, the hiccup matters less than the recovery. Never underestimate the tech gods' timing—or their flair for creative glitching.

I learned that preparation and how you respond make the difference between stumbling and sailing through. When you expect the unexpected, a "tech meltdown" can provide an opportunity to grow. I've become increasingly adept at adapting to whatever tech road bump pops up. This way, I keep my audience with me, rather than shaking their confidence when the platform misbehaves. A calm reset—what author and podcast host Mel Robbins calls "leave it and move on"—turns a disruption into just another beat in your talk. The key? Murphy's Law applies—everything that can go wrong will—so be ready.

Preparation means fewer "uh-oh" moments

You can't control your internet, surprise software updates, or garbled audio. But you can control your readiness. Proactive prep reduces your stress and keeps "uh-oh" moments from stealing your spotlight. Sometimes, preparation even turns them into "aha" moments.

Arrive 30–60 minutes early for big events; 5–10 minutes rarely covers real troubleshooting. If all's well, enjoy quiet focus time.

Here's my basic "tech insurance" checklist:

- **Run a pre-flight check:** lighting, camera, microphone, power cords, and Plan B options (spare headphones, internet hotspot).

- **Test your setup** at least 15 minutes before start time.

- **Shut down distractions:** unnecessary apps, browsers, tabs, and notifications.

- **Send materials** (slides, documents, polls) to a trusted colleague or host as a backup.

- **Post your "Tech-Day Ritual" checklist** where you'll see it or set it as your wallpaper.

A personal glitch save

Once, during a major client presentation, even after triple-checking everything, my breakout rooms refused to open. The "Open All Rooms" button was grayed out, likely a host/permission snafu after my brief disconnect. Rather than stall or apologize on a loop, I texted my wingperson—already set up as co-host—to start a quick discussion. He kept things moving while I regrouped and restarted the feature. Within two minutes, we were back on track. That simple backup plan saved the flow—and my focus.

If you're solo, quick recoveries:

- **Jump back in** via phone dial-in, secondary device, or hotspot.

- **Reassure participants:** "Thanks for hanging in—my WiFi went rogue, but I'm back."

- **If needed, post an ETA** in chat/text/Slack.

- **Send a "Reconnecting—back in 2 minutes" email,** possibly from your phone.

- **Deputize on the fly:** Ask, "Would someone paste the next agenda item in chat while I reset?" This strategy involves the group, keeps the meeting alive, and helps calm you, the presenter.

A tale of two presenters

🚫 Presenter A: The blank starer

You freeze mid-presentation after your tech fizzles and repeatedly mutter sorries, followed by a blow-by-blow walk-through of your troubleshooting as you open and close the same windows repeatedly—like pressing the elevator button multiple times, hoping the doors open sooner. As you click furiously, you duck out of sight. The audience stares blankly, productivity seeps away, and your credibility unravels with every awkward pause.

✅ Presenter B: The calm connector

"Looks like my internet needs a pep talk! Give me ten seconds as I reload." You smile, narrate your plan, and invite the audience to chat while you sort things out. Relatability, a touch of humor, and transparency tend to keep everyone rooting for you.

Reset in public: Communicate, don't flail

As Zandan (2020) suggests, maintaining warmth and steady body language helps sustain trust in virtual meetings, even when the tech falters. Inside, my reflex is to flail; outside, I inhale, exhale, and slow down, so my brain stays online while I troubleshoot. Name the issue, narrate one step, and keep moving. It's the tech—not you. Example: "Reloading now—back in 10 seconds." Pause, fix, ask for help if needed, then resume.

Research on online training shows that technical failures do more than frustrate—they can impair learning and increase dropout rates (Sitzmann et al., 2010). While meetings and presentations aren't identical to formal training, the lesson carries over: how you respond to a glitch helps protect engagement and effectiveness.

Tech troubleshooting exercise
Try these (30 minutes)

> **Challenge:** Deliberately create quick meltdowns—turn off your camera, unplug your mic, drop your connection, or "lose" your slides.
>
> **Solution:** Have a phone dial-in or second device ready for an instant switch.
>
> **Quick fix:** Practice recovery phrases such as "I'll be right back!"
>
> **Exercise:** Pretend your internet lags. Smile, narrate the steps, and calmly re-engage the audience.

Backup plan essentials (10 minutes)

> **Challenge:** You lose your connection mid-talk.

Solution: I often share my slides beforehand with a trusted colleague or host in advance.

Quick fix: Write down a one-sentence contingency script to manage expectations (e.g., "I'll reconnect in 30 seconds—if you lose me, I'll be right back!").

Exercise: Practice your recovery phrase for smooth transitions.

Bonus: Say it with a smile—mood is contagious.

Smooth screen sharing (10 minutes)

Challenge: Fumble or freeze mid-transition.

Solution: Open only what you need; close confidential files; label browser tabs clearly. Keep a clean desktop or share a single window to avoid surprise pop-ups.

Quick fix: Use preview/hide share mode before you go live

Exercise: Record and rehearse switching between camera and slides seamlessly.

Audio and video fails (10 minutes)

Challenge: Sound or camera failure at a key moment.

Solution: Keep backup mic, phone dial-in, or spare webcam ready.

Quick fix: Know your audio/video source switch and practice it.

Exercise: Practice simulated audio failure and recover calmly.

Mute/Unmute norms (and ab-norms!) (15 seconds)

Ask participants to mute when not speaking to reduce echo and crosstalk. Remember to unmute before you speak. Although a day isn't complete until someone reminds me to unmute. A sticky note or on-screen cue helps. Caveat: In live literary readings and performance-style events (e.g., author read-alouds), some facilitators leave mics on so reactions—laughter, snaps, claps—are audible.

State the norm upfront and switch to mute if background noise creeps in. Narrate your recovery: "I'm switching to my headset now—thanks for your patience!" This steadies you and reassures your audience.

🖥 Rookie mistakes—DON'T:

- Fail to have a backup plan or quick fix ready; DO take 15 minutes the day beforehand to assess what to do when Murphy's Law comes knocking on your tech door.
- Stare blankly or ramble when tech fails; DO take a deep breath and keep your audience informed.
- Use jargon or blame the platform; DO keep your language simple and your attitude positive.
- Go silent while troubleshooting; DO offer a one-line status update and a micro-task (poll or chat question) to keep engagement while you troubleshoot.
- Over-apologize; DO think Captain "Sully" Sullenberger, who safely landed US Airways Flight 1549 on the Hudson River after a bird strike disabled both engines—poise under pressure personified.

 In-person presentation strategies

No tech is foolproof. When presenting live, test everything early. If something fails, pivot with a smile—"Let's just talk through our main points!"—and keep your energy up. Just like with online presentations, I always enlist a "room wingperson" to jump in with logistics or slides if needed.

Facilitating online meetings

As a facilitator, clarify contingency plans upfront ("If we run into connection issues, here's what you can expect…"). Assign a backup host if possible. If things go haywire, invite the group to weigh in on chat, or use a poll to keep people engaged. Sometimes I'll joke about offering a prize for whoever makes contingency planning sound exciting—because like insurance, you only notice how crucial these plans are once you need them.

Remind everyone early where to find chat, phone numbers, or links to catch dropped participants. Being proactive and showing you're willing to ask for help calms the room and demonstrates real leadership.

Tech tools

- **Portable hotspots and phone dial-ins** for backup internet.

- **Test dial-in features.**

- **Mic and webcam diagnostics.**

- **Remote control or host hand-off** for screen sharing.

- **Noise suppression apps** (e.g., Krisp, NVIDIA Broadcast on compatible PCs).

- **Checklist apps** (Google Keep, Trello) for tech prep rituals.

- **Set up a recording safety net:** Use local (Zoom, Teams) or cloud (Zoom, Teams, Google Meet/Drive) recording so you don't lose your presentation if there's a dropout. Turn on auto-record when available and always let people know you're recording.

Introvert insights

If tech issues spike your stress, rehearse recovery phrases and allow yourself to pause and breathe. Audiences appreciate calmness more than perfection. Sometimes, your composed management of a glitch is the highlight.

Cultural considerations

Audience expectations for pausing, apologies, and troubleshooting disclosure vary. Understand your group's style. If uncertain, offer brief reassurance and proceed respectfully.

Picture this: Glitch, pause, recover

Three minutes into your virtual presentation, your slides freeze. You stop—not in panic, but on purpose. "Looks like my computer's taking a coffee break," you quip, clicking to the backup copy already open in another window. The audience chuckles.

Your lighting still flatters, your mic's still crisp, and your backup hotspot still keeps you online. Within 30 seconds, you're rolling again. The chat lights up—not with complaints, but with "Nice save" and "Wish I stayed that calm." By the end, they remember your message— and how you made a tech breakdown part of the show. You didn't just survive the disruption—you owned it.

Pro tip

Call a quick reset, like announcing a "take five" to let everyone stretch and regroup. When I have a wingperson, we send private messages or texts—sometimes those little lifelines are all you need to pull off a smooth save. A brief musical chime or even a joke can help everyone reset.

 The big idea

Expect tech glitches. Your audience remembers your response, not the glitch. Stay calm, show warmth and even a touch of humor, and move forward.

Next up—Chapter 7: Engage Your Audience

You'll discover practical strategies to make online meetings interactive, productive, and even enjoyable. Tools that help you stand out as an effective virtual facilitator await you in Chapter 7.

References

Sitzmann, T., Kraiger, K., Stewart, D., & Wisher, R. (2010). The comparative effectiveness of web-based and classroom instruction: A meta-analysis. *Personnel Psychology*, 59(3), 623–664.

Zandan, N. (2020, March 19). What it takes to run a great virtual meeting. *Harvard Business Review*.

Chapter 7

Engage Your Audience

You've polished your slides, practiced your delivery, and nailed your lighting. But halfway through your virtual presentation, you feel it: The audience has left the building. Or rather, they're still logged in but checking email, WhatsApp, or dinner recipes. Let's call it "digital exit syndrome." You can almost hear the tab-switching from where you sit. I've been there too, as a presenter and a participant, deflating as the energy drains from the Zoom space like a balloon losing helium. So, what's missing? It's not always a lack of content or charisma.

Zoom fatigue—a form of cognitive overload caused by prolonged eye contact, reduced nonverbal cues, and constant self-monitoring—plays a role in this digital exit syndrome. Addressing this, research by Bailenson (2021) identifies four main causes and proposed strategies to reduce mental strain, including taking scheduled breaks and hiding your self-view window. The special sauce is true audience engagement—a level of interaction that transforms listeners from passive observers into active participants. Sure, the term might sound buzzword-y because it's tossed around in business meetings as a must-have marketing metric. But the need for two-way interaction never gets old.

The power of engagement

For me, delivering an interactive presentation online is more natural than reciting a speech; it's a conversation, not a monologue. In a monologue, words go out, but nothing comes back, like speaking into a void. A successful presentation feels more like a dinner party and less like an info-dump. Everyone is at the table, sharing stories. When you invite interaction, you create genuine exchange. That's the charge in the virtual air that I thrive in, and what I hope to encourage with you, not just "talking at" but "talking with"—connecting, in real time.

In virtual spaces, what matters most isn't just what you say, but how you spark real interaction and build connection—so your audience is part of the action, not just viewers in the back row of a movie theater. I want you to picture your audience not as silent moviegoers, but as your co-conspirators.

Engagement has always mattered, but in today's Zoom-centered work world, it faces new challenges. So, ask yourself how to get your audience leaning in instead of checking out. And how much engagement is too much?

While engagement is crucial in all settings, it takes on special challenges in virtual environments. Zoom-like presentations are here to stay in a work world that spans time zones and cultures. So how do you get people to put down their phones (or at least pause Candy Crush) and join you? How do you spark involvement without overwhelming introverts or Zoom-fatigued meeting marathoners?

Recent research finds that well-structured virtual meetings improve employee focus, flow, and well-being through increased engagement and reduction of work-related fatigue (Rivkin et al., 2024). While their study centers on meetings, the findings can inform virtual presentations, which often occur within such settings.

As we explore engagement strategies, let's consider two contrasting approaches to virtual presentations.

A tale of two presenters

🚫 Presenter A: The monologuer

You push out a steady stream of facts, glued to your script, barely glancing up for input. The result? Your participants fade into the background, attention scattered, engagement gone.

✅ Presenter B: The interactor

You bring the chat into play, launch a poll, and toss out unexpected questions. The room lights up. Attention sharpens. Now, your audience isn't just physically present—they're actively in the moment, with you.

Find your engagement sweet spot

Features like polls and breakout rooms are your presentation spices—just enough adds flavor, but too much can overwhelm the meal. The goal? Only use the tools that make your listeners hungry for more.

See the Venn diagram: One circle represents what your audience needs or prefers; the other shows what you're best positioned to deliver with confidence and clarity. The overlap? That's your ideal engagement zone—where your message lands powerfully and connections happen naturally.

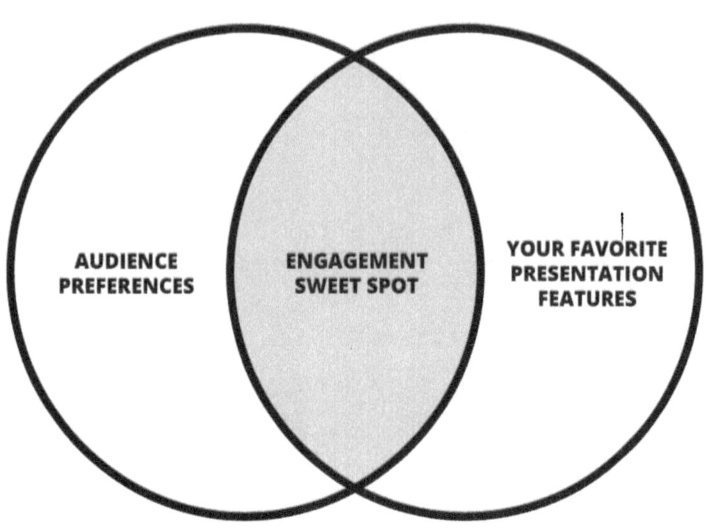

Left circle: What your audience prefers
Right circle: What you enjoy and excel at using
Overlap: Your engagement "sweet spot"

Not sure what your audience loves? Ask, don't assume. A quick survey or a note to organizers gives you clues—and helps you tune your session just right. Always check. Are your features enhancing your message—or turning into background noise? Engagement tools should spotlight your content, never drown it out.

Typical bells and whistles: Pros and cons

No single tool is a magic bullet. Choose tools to match your audience, your style, and your goals. Here's my quick-reference chart: what each tool brings and where it can trip you up. Before diving into specific tools, here's a quick guide to their strengths and potential pitfalls.

Engagement tool	Pros	Cons
Polls	Gauge opinions quickly; encourage participation	Can feel overused if not woven into content; technical glitches disrupt flow
Chat features	Enable real-time interaction; collect questions/comments	May be hard to track if chat volume is high
Breakout rooms	Build collaboration; energize small groups	Might make some participants uncomfortable; they consume valuable time to set up
Interactive visuals	Add variety and interest; promote hands-on learning	Requires practice to use smoothly; can distract if overused
Quizzes/Games	Reinforce learning while adding fun	May feel gimmicky or off-putting
Word clouds	Capture group input visually; provide instant snapshot	Oversimplify nuanced responses; limit expression
Collaborative whiteboards (Zoom, Teams, WebEx, Miro, Mural)	Support co-creation; foster brainstorming	Slow momentum if tech fails; challenge new users

Reaction emojis	Boost energy; provide quick feedback	Reduce interaction to shallow signals; vary by platform.
Annotations (Zoom/Teams built-in)	Invite audience to mark slides; enable instant collaboration on content	Create chaos if unmanaged; can be glitchy
Shared documents (Google Docs, OneNote)	Enable co-writing in real time; provide tangible takeaways	Require setup and comfort with the platforms
AI-enabled summaries	Record takeaways in real time; lighten note-taking load	Deliver errors if accuracy slips; require audience trust

No tool is intrinsically "good" or "bad." Use the pros and cons in this table as guideposts, not absolutes. By thoughtfully selecting and integrating these tools, you create a robust, engaging presentation without drowning out your message. Experiment to determine what works for different audiences and presentations.

Tailor strategies for your audience

Customize your approach. Some corporate audiences may appreciate quick polls, while some academic groups prefer deep discussions. Whatever you choose, keep the focus on relevance. Remember, knowing your audience's preferences helps you customize your approach.

"The audience is the most important component of every public speaking situation," according to research by Kroczek & Mühlberger (2023), who found in a virtual reality study that supportive audience cues—like nodding or smiling—directly enhanced speaker confidence and performance in real-life settings. The impact of such feedback likely extends to virtual presentations, where visible audience attentiveness can boost a presenter's confidence, while disengagement may increase anxiety.

Pacing matters

Break up your session with interactive moments every 10–15 minutes to keep attention high. Avoid clustering them together; space your touchpoints so people stay engaged rather than tune out.

Non-technical engagement (don't underestimate!)

While technical tools offer many opportunities, don't overlook traditional, proven methods to connect with your audience. These approaches ensure no one feels left out, regardless of platform or tech skills. Try the options below—and consider what else you or your colleagues have found effective to enrich your toolkit.

- **Storytelling:** Anchor ideas in personal anecdotes.
- **Show of hands:** Ask for quick input from small groups.
- **Humor:** Use it sparingly. A little light self-deprecation can put people at ease.
- **Metaphors and images:** Paint mental pictures to illustrate abstract ideas.
- **Q&A sessions:** Dedicate time for two-way interaction and deeper understanding.
- **Thought-provoking questions:** Spark debate and personal reflection.

Practice, test, and adapt

Before you dive in, review the "Typical Bells and Whistles: Pros and Cons" chart above to compare your options. Once you've chosen your engagement tools, use these tailored practice steps to set yourself—and your audience—up for success.

- **Polls:** Prepare and rehearse your poll questions in advance. Have a backup question ready in case your first doesn't land or a tech issue pops up.

- **Chat features:** Plan focused chat segments for key parts of your talk. If your audience is large or chat tends to scroll fast, assign a moderator to keep things on track and ensure voices are heard.

- **Breakout rooms:** Write out concise, clear instructions for each breakout activity. Practice saying them aloud so you sound confident and help participants understand what's expected.

- **Interactive visuals:** Prep all interactive slides and test your backup graphics in advance. Rehearse leading participants through the visual, highlighting how it supports your message.

- **Stories and analogies:** Craft a compelling two-minute story or analogy to humanize your content. Run through your delivery, timing yourself so it stays punchy and impactful.

Circle back to the Venn diagram and your engagement goals as you refine your approach. Consistent practice makes every tool more effective—and helps you handle surprises with confidence.

💻 Rookie mistakes—DON'T:

- Overload with too many features; DO keep it simple.

- Ignore audience feedback; DO listen and plan accordingly.

- Forget to explain interactive tools; DO be mindful that your participants may be at different tech levels.

- Use engagement techniques without a clear purpose; DO have an outcome in mind.

- Neglect to practice with chosen tools; DO practice until your presentation is "good enough," rather than its overrated enemy "perfect."

🎬 In-person presentation strategies

Much of what we've covered works in the physical world, too, plus:

- Adjust your voice and movement for the room.

- Use eye contact and gestures for emphasis (but don't pace nervously).

- Simple in-room check-ins ("Anyone ever notice this?") are just as powerful as virtual polls.

Remember, many principles translate between virtual and in-person—just adapt them for the environment.

Is it working? Measure and improve

After your talk, check:

- Chat activity
- Poll participation
- Feedback (don't assume it's coming; ask for it!)

Refine your approach every time. Use these measures to continuously improve your engagement, adapting to what works best for your audience.

Introvert insights

Introverts often prefer meaningful one-on-one conversations and may find large-group activities—like breakout rooms or rapid-fire discussions—more draining than engaging. As Furumo, de Pillis, and Green (2009) report, differences measured by the Big Five and the MBTI® instrument relate to trust and satisfaction in virtual versus face-to-face teams.

People lower in extroversion may show less immediate participation or comfort in fast-paced talk, especially when expectations are unclear. Research shows that agreeableness, conscientiousness, and extroversion predict higher levels of trust and satisfaction in virtual groups, while those lower in extraversion may value more structure and a pause to think before speaking.

I get that. As an introvert, I'm most comfortable in the facilitator role— listening, guiding, and playing air-traffic controller so everyone has space to contribute. But when I'm not facilitating and just participating, I prefer to be on the agenda with a clear role. That way I don't have to fight for airtime in an open discussion, which can feel like a full-contact sport.

So, what helps across styles? Two simple moves:

> (1) State the purpose, roles, and expected output for each activity.

> (2) Build in 3–5 minutes of solo think time before discussion.

Both raise participation without putting quieter folks on the spot, and they improve perceived team effectiveness for introverted and extroverted members alike (The Myers-Briggs Company, 2020).

Accessibility and cultural considerations

Pick components everyone can access. Text alternatives for visuals, screen-reader compatible platforms, humor that crosses cultures—these are musts in a Zoomed world. Being mindful keeps your sessions inclusive and respectful of diverse needs and backgrounds.

Picture this: The buzz, the nods, the "subterranean" high fives

Your slides are ready, your full coffee mug within reach. As participants log in, you kick things off with a playful poll, and instantly, the chat comes alive. Faces light up, "aha!" moments flash on camera, and you ride the wave of real-time feedback instead of presenting into a silent void. Every small engagement (polls, open questions, quick stories, or a shared whiteboard sketch) fuels a sense of momentum and togetherness. No guessing who's multitasking; you're all in it, actively creating value together.

Audience engagement feels different on the inside of an interactive session: chat buzzing, participants nodding in agreement, ideas sparking in real time. Those "subterranean" high fives—quiet affirmations and nods that ripple just below the surface—are the real pulse of an engaged audience.

Pro tip

Before your Q&A, plant a question (or two) with trusted participants or colleagues. If the audience is quiet or hesitant, you'll have an immediate prompt that breaks the ice, sparks discussion, and keeps energy high. This simple tactic takes the pressure off—and ensures you never face a wall of silence.

♀ The big idea

Audience engagement isn't about flash—it's about genuine connection. The best presenters invite participation, welcome feedback, and roll with surprises. Choose and blend your preferred mix of tools to create meetings people talk about and want to join again. Keep in mind that your style combined with purposeful engagement creates memorable experiences—ones your audience will look forward to.

Next up—Chapter 8: Shine, and Share the Spotlight

We'll explore how to boost your presence without hogging the stage—and how to make room for others while still standing out.

References

Bailenson, J. N. (2021). Nonverbal overload: A theoretical argument for the causes of Zoom fatigue. *Technology, Mind, and Behavior*, 2(1).

Furumo, K., de Pillis, E., & Green, D. (2009). Personality influences trust differently in virtual and face-to-face teams. *International Journal of Human Resources Development and Management*, 9(1), 36–58.

Kroczek, L. O. H., & Mühlberger, A. (2023). Public speaking training in front of a supportive audience in virtual reality improves performance in real-life. *Scientific Reports*, 13, 13968.

The Myers-Briggs Company. (2020). How personality influences virtual teamwork.

Rivkin, W., Moser, K. S., Diestel, S., & Alshaikh, I. (2024). Getting into flow during virtual meetings: How virtual meetings can benefit employee functioning in the work- and home domain. *Journal of Vocational Behavior*, 150, 103984.

Chapter 8

Shine, and Share the Spotlight

Increasing visibility isn't just a nagging "to do"— it can be rocket fuel for your career. When you increase your visibility, you're not just being seen, you're opening doors to new opportunities, collaborations, and recognition.

You've just nailed your online presentation. Your content captivated and your delivery was your personal best. But wait—don't vanish when it's over. Now's your chance to turn that talk into a visibility springboard to amplify your impact and let your expertise reverberate. The impact multiplies when you share the spotlight— because virtual success hinges more on inviting contributions than from slick delivery.

A tale of two presenters:

🚫 Presenter A: The invisible virtuoso

You've spent weeks crafting the perfect presentation. Your slides are works of art, your talking points are razor-sharp, and your expertise is unquestionable. But as you wrap up your talk, you simply close your laptop and call it a day. No social media posts, no follow-up emails, no snippets shared online. Your valuable content evaporates into the digital void, reaching only those who attended live. No one beyond the viral platform gets to bask in your brilliance. You've missed a golden opportunity to extend your reach and cement your authority.

 ## Presenter B: The visibility virtuoso

You've just delivered a knockout presentation. But instead of logging off, you're just getting started. You snap a screenshot of your virtual audience (yes, with permission), capturing the energy of the moment.

As soon as the session ends, you're crafting a punchy LinkedIn post, sharing key takeaways and tagging engaged participants. You extract a compelling quote from your talk and design a shareable graphic for X (formerly Twitter) and Instagram. You reach out to your company's internal communication team, offering to write a brief article for the newsletter based on your presentation.

Within hours, your 60-minute talk has transformed into a multiplatform visibility campaign, reaching far beyond your initial audience and showcasing your expertise to potential clients, collaborators, and employers.

Visibility workout and spotlight solutions
Try these (10 minutes)

Practicing these quick wins daily can turn visibility from a one-off spark into a lasting glow.

Visibility check (5 minutes)

> **Challenge:** Bucking your habit of keeping your value a secret.

> **Solution:** Develop a post-presentation visibility plan.

> **Quick fix:** Draft one key takeaway you could share on your preferred social media platform immediately after presenting.

Exercise: Sketch three rough social media posts highlighting different aspects of your recent presentation. (If you polish your posts, this exercise may take longer. For a quick workout, keep it rough and aim for 15 minutes' total.)

Spotlight sharing check (5 minutes)

Challenge: Focusing solely on self-promotion.

Solution: Identify and highlight contributions of others in your field.

Quick fix: Jot down one colleague or participant you could tag and thank for an insightful question during your presentation.

Exercise: Draft a brief LinkedIn recommendation for a co-presenter or panelist (keep it rough—you can polish later).

💻 Rookie mistakes—DON'T:

- Forget to follow up with engaged participants; DO follow up with a thank-you, link, or next step within a day.

- Drown your audience in self-promotion (e.g., self-aggrandizement, name-dropping, putting down others); DO state the result and evidence (metric, quote, link) and credit collaborators.

- Let visibility opportunities slip away—for you and your colleagues; DO capture and share one clip, one takeaway, and one tag (colleague/participant) within a day.

- Hide bragging behind false modesty; DO own your contribution plainly ("Here's what I did and what changed")—no hedging.

♟ In-person presentation strategies

The same principles apply off-screen, too. In-person presentations supercharge your visibility because they expand your presence into three dimensions. Instead of a webcam box, you have a whole room—your voice carries, your movements are seen from all angles, and your energy fills the space. Networking happens naturally before and after your talk: hallway chats, shared meals, impromptu introductions. These moments multiply your impact in ways a virtual meeting can't.

When you share the spotlight in person by inviting fellow panelists to expand on your points or zeroing in on an audience question, you create a visible generosity that others remember. Conferences especially magnify this effect: an insightful comment or a gracious nod to a colleague can ripple through an entire professional community. In the 3D world, sharing the spotlight often means getting it back many times over.

Facilitating online meetings

Seize opportunities to facilitate virtual meetings—they're a visibility goldmine. As a facilitator, you instantly become a go-to person with natural authority, no awkward self-promotion necessary. To make the most of this role, reach out beforehand and offer participants clear ways to chime in. Kick things off with a poll, a quick round robin (one sentence from each), or a chat prompt, and call people by name (with a ground rule that they can always say, "pass").

This isn't just about filling silence; it's about sharing the spotlight and making others visible alongside you. That dynamic ramps up your own visibility and builds real connection. Hale and Grenny (2020) have nailed some solid tricks for sparking engagement like well-timed prompts, shared responsibilities, breakout room tasks that keep energy up and participation genuine. Add these to your toolkit. You'll take your meetings to the next level, as places where people show up, speak up, and leave feeling truly heard.

Blending these engagement frameworks with a visibility mindset makes you not just an organizer but a connector and leader. You command the room without dominating it. And that is how you make your presence—and your peers' presence—unforgettable.

Tech tools

Harness digital allies to boost your visibility. Use LinkedIn Articles to expand on your presentation topics and showcase expertise to a wider professional audience. Create eye-catching graphics with Canva to share key points across platforms. Transcribe your presentations using Otter.ai for accessibility and repurposing. Record video summaries or follow-ups with Loom, adding a personal touch to your visibility efforts.

Introvert insights

For many introverts, visibility grows naturally from attentiveness: offering crisp summaries, asking thoughtful questions, and showcasing others' ideas. This approach invites quieter voices to be heard, without the pressure of hard-sell self-promotion.

Virtual presentations can be an ideal environment for this: active listening, concise synthesis, and generous crediting elevate you and your colleagues. Try reframing self-promotion as a form of service—share a brief takeaway, tag contributors, and post a quick recap to extend the conversation beyond the meeting.

If you're more extroverted, channel that energy into making space for others: Check in with quieter participants, offer them the floor, and tag collaborators in your follow-ups so more people are visible, not just you.

In virtual settings, structure beats polish—create engagement early (first-minute prompt, quick round robin, chat prompt) and keep the momentum going throughout. Speaking personally, stepping into a "performance" role—a presentation, panel, or class—feels natural; like many introverts, I enjoy the visibility, then recharge in solitude.

Accessibility and cultural considerations

Being an inclusive facilitator means ensuring everyone—not just the loudest voices—can fully participate. That means making your activities accessible, understandable, and welcoming to all.

Use platforms compatible with screen readers, provide text alternatives for visuals, and design activities that don't rely only on audio. Remember that humor, references, or idioms may not translate the same way across cultures and languages; keep your words and phrases simple and clear. Offer multiple channels for participation—chat, polls, hand raises, or verbal input—to accommodate different comfort levels and abilities.

Planning with inclusion in mind uplifts the group and shows respect for all participants. It's another way of sharing the spotlight that strengthens your leadership and your visibility by creating a welcoming space where every voice can be heard.

Picture this: Give and get

It's the closing minutes of a virtual panel you've orchestrated. Three industry experts you invited are spotlighted on screen, sharing insights that spark the chat. You're not just shining on your own—you've elevated your peers. Later, when those panelists repost clips and tag you, your visibility multiplies, more than you'll achieve on your own.

Pro tip

Create a visibility checklist for each presentation. Include pre-event promotion, day-of social media updates, and post-event follow-up actions. This systematic approach ensures you maximize every opportunity to shine.

♀ The big idea

Increasing your visibility in virtual settings isn't about hogging the spotlight—it's about illuminating your value. By making meaningful contributions, being meticulously prepared, and using digital tools effectively, you ensure your expertise shines through the screen.

The goal isn't just to be seen, but to be remembered for the quality of your insights and the generosity of your collaborations. As you implement these strategies, your virtual presence becomes a powerful asset—potentially surpassing the impact of in-person interactions. In the digital realm, your influence can ripple far beyond the confines of a single meeting or presentation.

Next up—Chapter 9: Prepare to Speak on the Spot

In the next chapter, we'll dive into techniques for impromptu speaking in virtual settings, equipping you to handle unexpected moments in the spotlight with poise and confidence.

References

Hale, J., & Grenny, J. (2020, March 9). How to get people to actually participate in virtual meetings. *Harvard Business Review*.

Chapter 9

Prepare to Speak on the Spot

Even when I show up well-prepared for an online presentation or meeting, one sharp, unexpected question can jolt me. Suddenly a heckler begins shouting inside my head, You don't know enough, you don't belong.

Yes, even after years of being in the hot seat, I still wrestle with that voice. But what helps me stay steady and keep going is not striving for perfection but noticing that inner critic, taking a breath, and pulling a few improv tools out of my pocket to stay present.

Maybe you can relate. An audience member fires off a pointed question. In that moment, you need to recover fast. On-the-spot speaking might not be your natural gift. As an introvert, it wasn't mine either, but it's a skill I've learned—and you can, too. With deliberate practice, you can respond effectively—even under the heat of the spotlight—and steer the presentation back to purpose. In the pages ahead, I'll share my favorite tools to help you find a smart, steady path where you won't lose your footing.

From inner doubt to improv tools

Improvisation skills aren't just for comedians or theater nerds— they're practical tools that help you adapt for rolling with punches, thriving in unpredictable moments, and bouncing back stronger from surprises (Koppett, 2013; Sawyer, 2011; Dudeck & McClure, 2018; Seppänen & Toivanen, 2023).

Think of improv skills as something you already practice daily. For example, imagine a water-cooler encounter at work: A colleague unexpectedly asks for help on a project you don't know much about. Instead of freezing, you respond, "Sure, I'd love to help. Let's see who else on the team can join us." This simple spontaneous language keeps collaboration on track and relationships positive—exactly what improvisation trains you to do.

Organizations back up this practical value. Research shows that improvisation exercises—like the key improvisational communication technique "yes, and"—don't just make meetings more fun, they build flexibility, creativity, and resilience. Psychological safety, which supports these outcomes, links measurably to better learning and innovation (Edmondson, 2019; Jin et al., 2024). Scholars argue that an improvisational mindset not only sparks better teamwork but also fosters workplaces where fresh ideas, safety, and adaptability thrive (Dudeck & McClure, 2018, 2021).

It might seem counterintuitive, but preparation underpins effective spontaneous speaking. By building a small toolkit of improv skills, you navigate unexpected moments with confidence. Studies find improv training reduces pre-performance stress and boosts interpersonal confidence (Seppänen, Makkonen, & Toivanen, 2020), while theoretical work explains how brain and body adapt through applied improvisation (Seppänen & Toivanen, 2023). Researchers and case studies also highlight improv's role in growing cognitive flexibility, emotional regulation, and adaptability (Seppänen & Toivanen, 2023; Dudeck & McClure, 2018). These are essential for on-the-spot speaking.

The "yes, and" technique serves as a simple but powerful tool that encourages you to accept others' ideas and build on them, rather than shutting them down. This behavior fosters creativity and collaboration when thinking on your feet, helping individuals and teams innovate and communicate more effectively. Applied improvisation experts note that this mindset helps professionals "surf the waves of unpredictable times," making it a crucial skill for leaders (McClure & Dudeck, 2021).

A tale of two presenters

🚫 Presenter A: The frozen fluster

A senior executive asks you an unexpected question with a stern tone and a scowl. You freeze. Your mind goes blank, and you stumble through an incoherent response. As self-consciousness sets in, you lose your audience's confidence, making it harder to recover. The remainder of your presentation feels like an uphill battle.

✅ Presenter B: The nimble navigator

Faced with the same question, tone, and scowl, you take a breath, acknowledge the value of the question, and smoothly transition into a relevant anecdote while formulating your response. This is my go-to method now—at least, when I remember to take that conscious breath! When I don't, well, I remind myself that I'm human. These techniques take practice, and I hope you'll give yourself the same grace.

Impromptu speaking toolkit
Try these (15 minutes)

Bridging technique (5 minutes)

> **Challenge:** Staying on message when faced with off-topic or difficult questions.

> **Solution:** Learn to bridge back to your key points with confidence.

Quick fix: Acknowledge the question, then redirect with a transition phrase.

How to use bridging effectively:

- First, acknowledge the question: "That's an interesting point..." or "I appreciate you bringing that up..."
- Then, bridge back to your main message: "What's important to remember is...," "That actually ties into a key takeaway...," or "While that's one perspective, another key aspect is..."

Exercise: Pick a random question (e.g., "What's your opinion on remote work?") and bridge to one key message (e.g., "Results improve when expectations and cadence are clear—weekly check-ins keep us aligned anywhere.").

Anecdote bank (5 minutes)

Challenge: Coming up with relevant examples on the spot.

Solution: Have a mental bank of versatile stories adaptable to different contexts.

Quick fix: Prepare three anecdotes showcasing your expertise, problem-solving, or leadership.

Exercise: Write down three stories and practice telling each in under 60 seconds.

"Yes, and" practice (5 minutes)

> **Challenge:** Building on unexpected ideas or questions, even when you don't fully agree.
>
> **Solution:** Use the "yes, and" technique to acknowledge and expand on what others say.
>
> **Quick fix:** Begin with "Yes, and..." to keep conversation flowing instead of shutting it down.
>
> **Exercise:** With a partner, take turns building a story one sentence at a time, each starting with "Yes, and..."

Answering tough questions on the spot

While you can prepare for about 80% of questions, the real test is handling the ones from left field. Here's how:

Buy time:

- Take a deliberate breath before responding.
- Sip water to gather thoughts.
- Acknowledge the question without rushing.
- Repeat or reframe the question.

Manage your response:

- Say what you know instead of dwelling on what you don't.
- Use tone, pacing, and pauses to stay composed.
- Offer to follow up if needed.
- Avoid unnecessary apologies.

Useful phrases:

- "That's a compelling question. My initial thoughts are..."

- "I haven't encountered that before, but I'll look into it and follow up."

- "Would you clarify what you mean?"

- "Before I answer, I'd love to hear what others think."

- "To keep us on track, let's follow up offline on that topic."

💻 Rookie mistakes—DON'T:

- Freeze in silence; DO acknowledge the question as you prepare.

- Apologize excessively for not knowing; DO show curiosity and interest in learning.

- Fill every pause; DO employ silence as a powerful tool.

- Ignore your body language; DO remember how much you can express without words.

- Ramble endlessly; DO make your point and stop talking.

🎬 In-person presentation strategies

- **Plant your feet:** When you're caught off guard by a question, grounding yourself physically— standing tall and steady—gives you a moment to regroup. In impromptu moments, this physical anchor helps slow your racing mind, project confidence, and gain a moment to organize your thoughts.

- **Move into the audience:** When a zinger comes your way, don't freeze at the lectern. Walking into the audience or stepping toward the questioner shifts the energy, signals openness, and buys you time to think. This improv-inspired move also flips the dynamic; you're not "on the spot"—you're owning the room and inviting a real exchange.

- **Use your full body:** In person, you're not limited by a webcam box. If an unexpected question demands a big idea or a bold answer, use an expansive gesture, a purposeful step, or even a pause to collect your thoughts. Physical expressiveness creates presence, signals "I'm handling this," and gives your brain an extra beat to catch up—a classic trick from stage improv.

- **Show up early to acclimate:** The best improv isn't made from a blank slate—it's about using whatever's around you. When you arrive early, walk the space and greet a few people. The more at home you feel, the less likely your mind will blank if you're suddenly called on.

- **Use eye contact as your anchor:** When you're put on the spot, eye contact becomes a grounding technique. It centers your attention, calms your nerves, and keeps you authentic even as your mind races. I remind myself I'm talking to a group of individuals, not one scary Cyclops. Pick a friendly face (or the back wall), let your gaze settle there, and begin. This simple anchor steadies your voice, tethers you to the present, and resets your confidence.

- **Channel nervous energy to stay present:** When you have to speak on the spot, your body may go straight into a "fight or flight" amygdala hijack. Psychology research shows that that reappraising that arousal as excitement—literally saying to yourself "I'm excited"—improves performance more than trying to "calm down" (Brooks, 2014). Acting with intention despite your anxiety can steady your focus and restore clarity almost instantly. This quick reframe pairs well with a single breath and a beat of silence before you respond.

Facilitating online meetings

Seek out opportunities to facilitate online meetings—they boost your visibility and leadership naturally, while giving you invaluable practice in speaking confidently on the spot. In the improv classes I took early in my career, I learned that facilitation is the perfect place to sharpen impromptu skills—because while you guide the conversation, you're not doing all the talking. I've found the real joy lies in setting the stage where others can express themselves fully and authentically.

When you must speak spontaneously as a facilitator, your ability to invite participation and keep the meeting flowing makes all the difference in holding the room's attention. This includes quick call-outs—briefly naming or inviting specific participants to speak—summarizing comments and smoothly transitioning between speakers. These moments of thinking on your feet, responding in real time, build your improv muscle and keep energy high while also inspiring others to find their confidence to speak up when it counts. These strategies can turn spontaneous moments into breakthroughs.

Tech tools

You don't need a script to get good at speaking on the spot—but you do need practice. Here are some digital tools and hacks that help you develop impromptu skills:

- **Online flashcards** (Anki, Brainscape): Create a personal "curveball question" deck. Write prompts like "Describe your biggest work win" or "Share your perspective on hybrid work," and practice answering in under a minute. This builds a habit of concise, organized thinking.

- **AI feedback tools** (Yoodli, Google Interview Warmup): Record responses to your flashcard prompts. These tools can analyze your pacing, clarity, and filler words—helping you see how you perform even when you're not prepared.

- **Screen and audio recorders** (Zoom, Loom): Hit record, answer a random prompt, and play it back. Self-review is awkward at first, but you'll quickly spot nervous habits and get more comfortable thinking out loud.

- **Liberating Structures app** (LiSA): The LiSA app, developed by the Liberating Structures community, includes step-by-step guidance for 33 microstructures — many of which are improv-based or improvisation-friendly. Use it as a portable prompt library or workshop companion when you want to riff, bridge, or pivot in live conversations.

Choose the mix that fits your style and schedule and set a recurring calendar reminder to practice. As your mental reflexes get sharper, you'll rely less on panic and more on presence and composure.

Introvert insights

My journey: From tongue-tied to improv-proficient

During my 12 years on Wall Street, a Myers-Briggs Type Indicator® assessment confirmed I was an introvert—the thinking-before-speaking type. It explained my struggles in extroverted, fast-paced meetings.

I survived painfully early Monday meetings (after insomnia on Sundays!). Once, my extroverted boss stopped me in the hallway asking me to summarize the jargon-filled and complex meeting she missed. Cue the internal scramble.

I learned to buy time while projecting confidence: "Yes, I'd love to catch you up on that. I'll email you a summary this afternoon."

My ultimate secret weapon? Improv.

The "yes, and" technique I learned in improv classes wasn't about being funny—it taught me to trust myself to respond positively in the moment. Improvisation has taught me the collaborative habit of building on what I see and hear, even under pressure, which has been pivotal in my career.

Accessibility and cultural considerations

Make your impromptu speaking accessible to everyone by using clear, straightforward language free from jargon, idioms, or culturally specific references that might confuse people who speak English as an additional language. In on-the-spot speaking, clarity is your ally— especially when you don't have time to explain complex phrases.

Select meeting platforms and tools that support screen readers, offer captioning, and provide multiple ways to engage—chat, polls, hand raises, or speaking aloud—so participants with different abilities and comfort levels can join in fully. Ensure visuals have descriptive text and speak clearly to help those relying on captions or interpreters. Making these choices before and during your spontaneous moments creates a welcoming stage where everyone's voice matters and helps you stay connected even when thinking on your feet.

Respect cultural differences by avoiding humor or expressions that might not translate well across languages and cultures. Keep your words simple and universal and offer varied participation channels to honor different communication styles and preferences. When you approach your spontaneous remarks and responses with accessibility and cultural sensitivity at the forefront, you build trust, minimize misunderstandings, and amplify engagement—key to staying composed and confident on the spot.

Picture this: Calm with the curveball

You're deep into your quarterly update when your boss's boss fires off a question you didn't see coming. Instinctively, your pulse jumps. But instead of spinning out, you buy a few seconds with a deep breath and a sip of water. "That's a compelling question," you say, acknowledging his concern.

As you gather your thoughts, you glance at your notes, remembering that killer anecdote from last month's project win. With just a few seconds of pause, a quick comment to buy you time, and a touch of confidence, you deliver a clear answer that connects back to your main message. That bridge keeps you in control of the narrative. The result? Heads nod, the chat lights up, and afterward a colleague pings: "You sound so unflappable. How do you do it?" That's the real power of impromptu speaking: not sounding perfect, but present, real, and ready.

Pro tips

- **Pause before speaking.**

  A moment of silence feels longer to you than to the audience. Use that pause to collect your thoughts.

- **Start with a simple, clear structure.**

  Use the PREP model:

  - **Point:** State your main idea in a single, plain sentence.

  - **Reason:** Explain why it matters.

  - **Example:** Provide a quick illustration.

  - **Point:** Reinforce your key takeaway.

- **Keep your first sentence simple**.

  If you get flustered, start with:

  - "That's an insightful question."

  - "Let me take a moment to think about that."

  - "One key idea that comes to mind is..."

- **Practice unexpected questions.**

  Use friends or flashcards with random questions. Record yourself answering, review, repeat.

♀ The big idea

Mastering impromptu speaking isn't about changing who you are—it's about owning your strengths and trusted techniques. With practice, those nerve-racking curveballs become breakthrough moments when your agility, expertise, and composure take center stage. (And if you're like me, when you're tackling tough moments head-on, facing the fire, you might imagine a whiff of roasting marshmallows—a mental spark that grounds you and reminds you to breathe and find joy amid the heat.)

Next up—Chapter 10: Ace Virtual Meetings and Interviews

Virtual meetings are here to stay, but many find them draining. Join me in the next chapter and discover how to lead and participate in virtual meetings that are productive, interactive, and yes, enjoyable. We'll cover how to spark engagement, reduce distractions, and create inclusive spaces where everyone can shine online.

References

Brooks, A. W. (2014). Get excited: Reappraising pre-performance anxiety as excitement. *Journal of Experimental Psychology: General*, 143(3), 1144–1158.

Dudeck, T. R., & McClure, C. (Eds.). (2018). Applied improvisation: Leading, collaborating, and creating beyond the theatre. *Bloomsbury Methuen Drama*. ISBN 9781350014350.

Dudeck, T. R., & McClure, C. (Eds.). (2021). The applied improvisation mindset. Bloomsbury.

Edmondson, A. C. (2019). The fearless organization: Creating psychological safety in the workplace for learning, innovation, and growth. Wiley. ISBN 9781119477242.

Jin, H., Ma, M., & Lee, Y. (2024). The impact of team psychological safety on employee innovative performance: Communication behavior as a mediator. *PLOS ONE*, 19(10), e0306629.

Koppett, K. (2013). Training to imagine: Practical improvisational theatre techniques for trainers and managers. Stylus Publishing. ISBN 9781579220479.

Sawyer, R. K. (2011). Explaining creativity: The science of human innovation (2nd ed.). Oxford University Press. ISBN 9780199737574.

Seppänen, S., Makkonen, T., Toivanen, T., Jääskeläinen, I. P., Anttonen, M., & Tiippana, K. (2020). Effects of improvisation training on student teachers' behavioral, neuroendocrine, and psychophysiological responses during the Trier Social Stress Test. *Adaptive Human Behavior and Physiology*, 6, 356–380.

Seppänen, S., & Toivanen, T (2023). Improvisation in the brain and body: A theoretical and embodied perspective on applied improvisation. *Nordic Journal of Drama Research*, 12(1). ScholasticaHQ.

Chapter 10

Ace Virtual Meetings and Interviews

Group meetings, virtual or otherwise, often leave me a bit uneasy—topsy-turvy, even brain-freezy. Keeping pace is the hardest part; the tempo can feel more roller derby than roundtable. Hugging the rail, I try to slip in cleanly. I push myself to interject (interrupting's gentler sibling) and get a word in before the next person or topic barrels past.

This chapter shows you how to set the pace as a facilitator and participate with presence by tuning in to your verbal and nonverbal skills and virtual controls. I've distilled my experience into practical steps you can use right away.

Stretching beyond comfort

When I was researching my first book, *Self-Promotion for Introverts*, I took on a stretch assignment. I lined up at dawn for a spot in the overflow room at Berkshire Hathaway's annual meeting, hoping my question for CEO Warren Buffett would reach the main room. I asked for his advice for introverts on raising their visibility at work.

Buffett's answer stuck with me. As a young man, he was so anxious about public speaking that he dodged any class that required it. He eventually took a Dale Carnegie course to push through the discomfort and later taught at a university. Buffett's point: Communication is a skill you can develop, and school rarely prepares you for it. Stretching beyond my comfort zone provided me a life-long lesson.

You don't need to be a billionaire to learn to be heard. How? Practice. Take every opportunity you can to speak, online and in person. Facilitate when you can; participate with intention when you can't. Let's focus on real-world ways to show up, speak up, and stay present—without pretending to be someone you're not or letting meetings run your day.

A tale of two facilitators

🚫 Facilitator A: The chaos captain

You start late while admitting people one by one from the waiting room. Tech issues multiply: Your mic echoes, screen share doesn't work, notifications ping nonstop. You skip the agenda, let the loudest voices dominate, and the meeting ends late in utter confusion. Action items? Unclear. Everyone leaves frustrated.

✅ Facilitator B: The calm conductor

You log in as early as you need for a mic/camera/screen-share check, greet people by name, turn on captions and recording (with consent), set expectations, and assign clear roles (timekeeper, tech wingperson, notetaker—or delegate notetaking to an AI assistant). You post the agenda and links in the chat, use the "raise hand" feature to sequence speakers, invite quieter voices in, and break into smaller groups with a clear prompt and timer when useful. Everyone leaves feeling seen, engaged, and informed.

A tale of two online meeting participants

🚫 Participant A: The invisible presence

You join from a noisy space, camera off, screen name still "iPhone." You barely speak and when you do, it's off topic. You multitask and miss key points in the chat. You leave as invisible as you arrived.

✅ Participant B: The quiet contributor

You join a few minutes early with your camera on and audio checked, agenda open. You offer timely comments, support the conversation, use the chat and reactions to engage, and follow up thoughtfully— maybe with a direct message: "creative solution," "insightful point," or "well put." You amplify others' voices, too.

Same meeting, different impact. You choose how to show up.

Set yourself up for success

Tips for everyone, whether you're running the show or just showing up:

- Arrive early for a tech check, to settle in, and even build rapport with the early birds.

- Keep your background uncluttered and set up good lighting (lamps or ring lights in front).

- Set your camera at eye level.

- Dress and groom in a way that helps you feel your best and most confident.

- Keep agendas crisp, rotate speakers, include short breaks, and end five minutes early.

Zoom fatigue is real. As Bennett et al. (2021) found, video calls can be more exhausting than audio or in-person meetings. Fosslien & Duffy (2020) also highlight this fatigue and suggest design strategies to reduce strain in online meetings.

Taking the dread out of being on camera

Virtual meetings can trigger self-consciousness for even the most seasoned professionals. If seeing yourself onscreen leads to avoidance or anxiety, adjusting your setup can help: Frame your face clearly, experiment with lighting, and use "hide self-view" to minimize distraction. Practicing with friends, or AI tools, lets you rehearse and receive feedback in a low-pressure environment. Over time, even reluctant participants feel more present and poised, and may receive positive feedback on their increased visibility.

Be an inclusive and effective facilitator

Send the agenda 24–48 hours ahead, being mindful of participants in different time zones. Open with a 30-second preview, and assign clear roles (timekeeper, tech wingperson, notetaker—or AI can capture notes). Build in informal chitchat time, enable live captions or real-time translation for greater inclusion, and use meeting assistants to automate notes and tasks. Start by listening to the room and gently balance participation—invite quieter voices in and redirect long-winded speakers. Stay alert to nonverbal cues and check in if someone looks disengaged. Follow up with summaries and next steps.

Make an impact as a participant

- Prepare a point, question, or supportive comment in advance.

- Use straightforward language—jargon doesn't always land across teams and cultures.

- Interject respectfully: Raise your hand, say the speaker's name, or use segues like "Building on that..." and "I'd like to add..."

- Follow up in writing if you don't get to speak.

- Engage with the chat and reaction emojis (to amplify others, write "Building on Priya's point..." or "Seconding Priya's proposal...").

- Need an entry line? Try: "Quick add...," "Another angle to consider is...," or "Here's a risk to flag..."

- Experiment with fun ways to chime in: "I have a crazy idea..." (Often, others will gladly run with it!)

Practice interjecting

Challenge: You can't find a clear opening.

Solution: Use a visual cue (e.g., hand raise or wave) or say someone's name.

Quick fix: Keep handy phrases like "That brings to mind ..." or "My favorite part of that idea is ..."

Exercise: Role-play with friends or an AI tool, trying quick, respectful entries into the discussion.

Practice managing an over-sharer

Challenge: Someone can't stop talking or going on tangents.

Solution: Have phrases ready: "Thanks, Jordan. Let's hear from someone who hasn't spoken yet" or "I'm mindful of the time. Would you summarize your point in one sentence?"

Quick fix: Smile and bring things back: "Thank you for sharing. We need to return to the agenda now."

Exercise: Practice redirecting in a mock meeting. Review tone and body language—AI tools like Fireflies.ai and Equal Time can help you track who talks, for how long, and whether participation is balanced. Use these insights to identify over-sharers and fine-tune your facilitation.

Practice handling virtual head-butting

Challenge: Someone criticizes or shames another participant.

Solution: Create and share ground rules beforehand; if tension builds, pause the meeting, acknowledge the disagreement, and restate the goal.

Quick fix: Jump in: "Let's focus on the issue, not the person."

Exercise: Simulate conflict resolution (with a friend or AI); practice depersonalizing the conflict ("I'm hearing you say...") and steering back to the agenda.

💻 Rookie mistakes—DON'T:

- Log in late and unprepared; DO show up early to be ready for anything.

- Skip your tech check; DO give yourself enough time in case you have to shoo away the tech gremlins.

- Look away while speaking; DO keep returning to the camera to connect better with others.

- Multi-task with distracting tabs; DO join from a clean desktop.

- Ramble or use unclear jargon; DO make every word count.

- Use busy backgrounds or poor lighting; DO show your best professional image.

🪑 In-person presentation strategies

When meeting in person, scout the space and test the tech ahead of time. Greet people warmly, make eye contact, and use natural gestures to build rapport.

Hybrid & hy-flex (quick guide)

Hybrid meetings mix in-person and remote attendees; hy-flex aims for fully equal live participation across both. To keep one conversation, route all audio through the room system; require mics for in-room speakers; appoint a "remote advocate" to watch chat/hands; default to shared artifacts (live docs/whiteboards); and time-box turns so remote voices don't get buried. See Chapter 5 for more tactics and definitions.

Research from Microsoft (2025) shows that managing meeting rhythm and responsibilities is vital to hybrid team engagement and to prevent the "infinite workday"—in which meetings bleed endlessly into evenings, and remote participants risk being sidelined. Applying these practices ensures everyone's voice and attention are captured, no matter where they work.

Tech tools

Helpful tools include Otter.ai for live captions, Zoom polls, and breakout rooms, collaborative notes in Google Docs or a similar platform, and timer apps to keep things on track. AI assistants can streamline transcripts and action items, freeing your focus for people. For greater accessibility, I use features like live captions. One client uses Otter.ai to help all participants—including those with hearing differences—stay fully engaged.

Introvert insights

Even after years of experience, my mind can go blank when put on the spot. See Chapter 9 for more about impromptu speaking. It helps to remember that you don't need all the answers right away. I've learned that my quiet nature can be an asset, especially with tools and prep. It brings calm and steadiness, leveling the playing field in fast group settings.

When I'm expecting a brainstorming session, I think of a few ideas in advance—otherwise, collaborative ideation sessions can drain my battery. I also use chat when I have something to contribute without breaking the flow. Sometimes, I prefer to share my ideas after a meeting by email.

Preparation brings calm; improvisation keeps you responsive (Ancowitz, 2025; University of Michigan, 2020). Collecting stories and bridging phrases ("What matters is…") and using the power of a thoughtful pause help me stay present. Good enough beats invisible, every time.

If you're an introvert, prepare a few points in advance and challenge yourself to use them early in the meeting. According to the *Harvard Business Review* (2024), visibility for introverts is best cultivated through thoughtful preparation and intentional early participation.

If you tend toward extroversion, try the guardrails below.

Extrovert insights

- Channel your energy into structure: Open with a concise headline, then yield the floor.

- Pause on purpose: Build 3–5-second beats into your speaking so others can enter.

- Keep it bite-size: Cap comments at 45–60 seconds before inviting another voice.

- Use the chat to amplify others (e.g., "Building on Jon's point…").

- If you're facilitating, time-limit brainstorms and call on people by name to balance participation.

Accessibility and cultural considerations

Make sure your virtual meetings and interviews are accessible to all participants. Choose platforms that support captions, interpreters, and screen readers, and share materials in advance in formats that are easy to open and review. Speak clearly, avoid rushing, and describe visuals so that everyone can follow along.

Respect cultural differences in how people participate. In some cultures, pausing before speaking signals thoughtfulness; in others, quick interjections are expected. Humor, idioms, and gestures may not translate well across cultures, so keep language clear and neutral. By planning for accessibility and showing cultural sensitivity, you set the stage for conversations where everyone can contribute fully.

Virtual interview essentials

Virtual interviews share many principles with online meetings but add a few twists. Some video interviews give you only seconds to prep and 2–3 minutes to respond, and without live interaction.

Before you record (one-way video)

Rehearse with tools like Zoom, Loom, Yoodli, or Big Interview. Practice looking into the camera, speaking with energy, and pausing naturally between thoughts. Some companies also use AI scoring; use your trial runs with these tools to keep your answers clear and concise, and authentically you. Try Google's Interview Warmup platform for practice prompts and feedback.

During a live interview

- **Treat it as a conversation:** Listen actively, nod, and ask smart follow-up questions.

- **Answer with structure:** Headline → one proof point → brief example → close the loop.

- **Be succinct:** Finish answers in 45–60 seconds, then say something like "Happy to share more details."

- **Set up your space:** Keep brief notes handy but avoid reading word-for-word unless you can deliver it naturally; always nail the basics, like good lighting, eye-level camera, and minimal distractions.

- **Build rapport fast:** Use vocal warmth, tight stories, and polished openings; research shows the brain forms impressions from voices almost instantly (Lavan et al., 2024).

Personally, I'm relieved that I'm not job hunting. The thought of getting an initial interview screening with a faceless robot, something many of my clients and grad students endure, makes me gulp hard. But still, if I had to do it, I would remind myself to prepare sufficiently so I can just be me in front of the camera. How about you?

Holographic meetings: A peek at the future

Imagine stepping into a meeting where the person you're talking to isn't just a flat image on a screen but appears right there in the room with you—life-sized, in three dimensions, and making eye contact as naturally as if they were sitting across the table. This is not science fiction; it's the future of virtual meetings already taking shape.

I first caught a glimpse of this sci-fi reality on Lex Fridman's podcast, where he had a holographic conversation with Google CEO Sundar Pichai. The not-so-secret tech? Google Beam (formerly known as Project Starline), a groundbreaking system that uses six cameras, spatial audio, and adaptive lighting to create a stunningly realistic 3D image without the need for headsets or glasses.

Thanks to a collaboration with HP, the first commercial version of this technology—called the HP Dimension—is now available, though it carries a price tag of around $25,000 (Bonk, 2025). But what you get is extraordinary: a 65-inch light field display that tricks your brain into perceiving real depth and presence, coupled with AI that transforms traditional video streams into immersive holograms.

Remember when video conferencing felt futuristic? Soon, immersive telepresence like this might be just as common and just as easy as hopping on a Zoom call today. The technology is designed to make remote conversations feel as natural and connected as in-person ones, bringing subtle cues like eye contact and body language back into the conversation.

For those of us who have been captivated by the promise of virtual meetings but exhausted by flat, lifeless video feeds, this peek into the future is thrilling. It's not just about cooler tech; it's about transforming the way we collaborate, connect, and communicate.

Recap: Your action steps for virtual presentations, meetings, or job interviews

- **Arrive poised and prepped:** Test your tech, set up your space, check your audio and camera, and review the agenda before you join.

- **Engage with intention:** Listen closely, use the chat and reactions, and aim for active (not passive) participation.

- **Amplify all voices:** If you're an extrovert, consciously invite quieter colleagues into the conversation; if you're an introvert, prepare a few points and challenge yourself to use them.

- **Experiment often:** Try new tools—AI assistants, live captions, breakout rooms, hybrid/hy-flex features—to find what helps you connect and collaborate best.

- **Embrace imperfection:** Presence and willingness matter more than polish. Show up as your best real self, ready to contribute, learn, and grow.

- **Remember:** Every online encounter—whether you're leading, participating, interviewing, or brainstorming—is a fresh opportunity. Connection, clarity, and a dash of fun will always win the day.

Picture this: Skillfully weaving every voice into a vibrant fabric of connection

A buzzing calendar alert. You're logging on, just a little nervous—a new project team, fresh voices. The meeting starts: the facilitator posts the agenda, names a notetaker, and smiles. You tweak your camera, check your lighting, and angle yourself for the best framing. With a pause, you jump in: "Quick add..." Conversations flow, gentle as jazz, not a stampede. Someone uses the chat to second your point. As ideas build, you spot a quiet voice and amplify: "Building on Lee's point..."

Afterward, you send a quick follow-up celebrating a bright idea. The AI summary arrives, crisp and clear—everyone's contributions tracked and action items set. You close your laptop energized; you've artfully facilitated the conversation—onscreen and in real time.

This isn't just another virtual meeting. It's a chance to be heard, to try new tools, to bring out your quiet insights, or sharpen your focus. You've learned to treat the digital space as less of a hurdle than a canvas—a place to experiment, improvise, and stretch your skills a little further.

Pro tip

Share the spotlight by recognizing others' input in the moment—this builds trust, energizes the group, and amplifies involvement. Use the improv tool "yes, and..." from Chapter 9 to keep participation lively and collaborative.

☍ The big idea

You don't need to be a TV anchor or an influencer to have impact. Show up prepared, stay engaged, and be intentional with your participation.

Final thoughts

What if your next online meeting or presentation wasn't something to dread but an opportunity to connect, be heard, and maybe even have a little fun? You've earned the skills and the confidence to show up as the voice who nudges the conversation in new directions, the facilitator who gives others space to shine, or the interviewee who brings preparation and personality. Not every answer needs to sparkle—sometimes a quick, off-the-wall idea sparks the best discussion.

Each virtual moment is also a chance to experiment with tools—from live captions and AI meeting assistants to teleprompters and, someday, holographic meetings. Why not go from brain fog to creative collaboration? The best part? Every online encounter is a chance to bring more of yourself and influence your world from wherever you are. It's also an opportunity to inform, inspire, persuade, and connect with others.

So, take a breath, welcoming your true self to shine through. Repeat to yourself, "Presence beats polish." Your next chapter starts now— one meeting and presentation at a time. I'm rooting for you.

References

Ancowitz, N. (2025, July 15). Prep meets improv: A toolkit for introverts. *Psychology Today*.

Bennett, A. A., Campion, E. D., Keeler, K. R., & Keener, S. K. (2021). Videoconference fatigue? Exploring changes in fatigue after videoconference meetings during COVID-19. *Journal of Applied Psychology*, 106(3), 330–344.

Bonk, L. (2025, June 11). The first Google Beam device is the $25,000 HP Dimension. *Engadget*.

Fosslien, L., & Duffy, M. W. (2020, April 29). How to combat Zoom fatigue. *Harvard Business Review*.

Harvard Business Review. (2024, March 6). An introvert's guide to visibility in the workplace.

Lavan, N., Burston, L. F. K., Knight, S., McGettigan, C., Garrido, L., Belin, P., & Kriegeskorte, N. (2024). The time course of person perception from voices in the brain. *Proceedings of the National Academy of Sciences*, 121(7), e2318361121.

Microsoft. (2025, June 17). Breaking down the infinite workday. *Microsoft WorkLab*.

University of Michigan. (2020, April 15). No kidding: Theater improv makes you happier, creative, tolerant of uncertainty. *Michigan News*.

Acknowledgments

Writing a book about online presentations is a little like hosting one: It takes energy, preparation, and more than a few do-overs. I've been teaching these skills at NYU and to clients, and much of what's here comes from shared exploration, trial, and generous feedback from audiences who helped refine these ideas in real time.

Deep gratitude to Mike Barlow—writer of dozens of books, mentor and word-wise consigliere—who changed my trajectory when I was about to self-publish this manuscript. Mike actually picked up the phone, and I actually answered it. For a book about online presenting, that was almost rebellious.

Just as the fall semester was looming, he invited me to launch this book as the inaugural title with the new University of Bridgeport Press, and here we are. Mike, thank you for seeing the book's potential and for believing in its value for university students and professionals alike.

Mike, thank you also for introducing me to the incredible Randy Laist, PhD, professor and chair of English at the University of Bridgeport and author of *Rethinking Writing Instruction in the Age of AI*. Randy, we are kindred spirits, and I'm grateful for our seamless partnership; you and Mike have been the bedrock of my A team in making this book happen.

Heartfelt thanks to Suze Allen, my editor and book doula, who midwifed this project with wisdom, patience, and grit. You helped me cut through clutter and kept me grounded when my mind started wandering to unhelpful but well-trodden ground. I'm also grateful to the many members of Suze's writers' community—her moxie-ful band of muses—whose camaraderie, laughter, and candor made this process lighter and brighter.

Appreciation to Kathryn Britton for her thoughtful early reads and steady encouragement across drafts. You helped me clarify the big picture while fine-tuning the details. I also thank members of Kathryn's writers' community for their feedback, positive-psychology-infused appreciation for research, and warmth—especially those who sparked new ideas across cultures and time zones.

Deep thanks to Nil Demircubuk, PhD, whose open-hearted presence and camaraderie have meant the world, and to Senia Maymin, PhD, whose joy and generosity are infectious. Senia interviewed me for her video podcast early in the book's development, bringing her characteristic curiosity, deep intelligence, and playfulness. I'm so grateful to have shared this book's journey with you both.

Other writers and artists who deserve special mention include Basi Perkins, Aren Cohen, Jan Stanley, Rosie Hancock, Lisa Provost, Jeanne Drevas, Anne Fizzard, Ilene Schaffer, MAPP, MA, PCC, Sarah Pletts, Leigh Strimbeck, Janet Kenney, Caroline Ceniza-Levine, Drew Alexander, Peter Welch, Jen Babcock, Hank Kimmel, Sid Efromovich, Happy Mason, Melodie Sommers, Sarah Ford, Barbara Bellman, and Margaret Shepard.

Special shout-out to Roland Tec, who co-hosted a writers' workshop with Suze Allen that fueled tremendous encouragement and inspiration for this project. Gratitude with a big G to Anne Newgarden, who invited me to join her for a shared reading from my manuscript and her book *Adventures of a Soul* on the Jersey Shore. Anne brought a spirited gaggle of friends and family, whose warmth and enthusiasm made the evening unforgettable—and I'm grateful for the support of her dear friend Linda Stults Myers, who cheered us both on.

Acknowledgments

I'm endlessly grateful to Ross Brand, livestreaming pioneer and generous creative force, for his enduring support and for reminding me that technology and humanity can, and must, coexist gracefully on screen.

To the many clients, colleagues, and graduate students I've learned from over the years, you've each left your mark in countless ways. You've kept me sharp, curious, and always experimenting.

Warm thanks to MJ & Barry, Rich & Ellen, Allie, Jonny, Val, Pam & Tomer, Joe, and Benny, whose endless punning and spontaneous asides during family Zooms remind me that connection doesn't depend on perfect timing or even on flawless muting. And to GMM and the late AA, who set the standard for speaking up long before Zoom made it fashionable. Their unfiltered honesty still echoes in my head and in my better punchlines.

I've also been fortunate to have the steadfast encouragement and insight of Karen Abrams Gerber, EdD, Anastasia (Natassa) Boukouvala, Carol Abrams, Monica Glina, EdD, Hermina (Nina) Batson, Shraddha Wanage, Moira Shaughnessy, Amy Byun, Anuradha J. Cetta, Marjorie Ramos, Sheyla Ramos, Jenilee Ramos, Vanessa Esparza, Steve Gogel, Janet Rosen, Marianna Lead, Roger Kastner, Bryan Chandler, Ying Shiau, Elaine Ahlberg, Dana Kaplan, Paul Rátz de Tagyos, Caitlin McClure, Hope King-Gilbert, Sophia Glezos Voit, Ariane Saney, Cornelia Lévy-Bencheton, Christine Fischer, Fernanda Garcia, Stephanie Cziczo, Stephanie Mieras Hansen, SPHR, SHRM-SCP, and Vincent Suppa. Also, the beloved Team Fred Burke from one of my enduring and favorite stomping grounds (Baruch Zicklin CUNY GCMC and so forth): Deborah Butler, Justyn Makarewycz, Lindsey Plewa, Jack Pullara, Annie Himmelsbach, Jennifer Seidman, Ellen King. Hats off to Greg Leporati and Carson Billingsley for being incredible collaborators, too; ditto Janet Rossbach for repeatedly welcoming me to another favorite stomping ground. Perspectives from all of you, each distinct and hard-won, remind me that communication thrives on collaboration.

Finally, to the remarkable professionals who contributed blurbs for this book—your insights, generosity, and belief in me mean the world to me. I'm deeply grateful for your vote of confidence and honored to be in your company.

It takes a village to write a book, just as it takes a team to run a meeting or class. This one's for all of you who made me a better thinker, presenter, and educator—along the way. Here's to the power of words, the courage to share them, and the people who keep us talking.

About the Author

Nancy Ancowitz is a career strategist and career director at NYU. She is the author of *Self-Promotion for Introverts* (2009) and *Business Writing: Say More with Less* (2024). Her work has been published in *The New York Times* and *The Wall Street Journal*, and she blogs for *Psychology Today* and The *Times of Israel*.

For more information, visit nancyancowitz.com.

www.ingramcontent.com/pod-product-compliance
Lightning Source LLC
Chambersburg PA
CBHW030054110726
47973CB00002B/15